"If you have had theological concerns for the excesses and lack of balance and biblical basis for the inner healing/deliverance ministries, as I have had, you will find this book a refreshing and corrective contribution to the much-needed ministry of pastoral care. It overlaps with my conviction to equip the layperson to do the work of ministry and to adjust our methods to include God as the Wonderful Counselor."

—**Dr. Neil T. Anderson**, founder and president emeritus,
Freedom in Christ Ministries

"Paula and I have been honored as the pioneers of inner healing. But many have said our writings are too deep and complex for the untrained. A great need has long existed for someone to reduce inner healing to simpler, everyday language and tools. Our friend Andy Reese has done that admirably in his book *Freedom Tools*. I heartily recommend using it to help laypeople minister via 'Sozo' to each other."

—**John Loren Sandford**, co-founder, Elijah House Ministries

"Baggage. I am convinced that most Christians fail to become dynamic and effective ambassadors for Christ because they carry with them heavy loads of emotional baggage stuffed with years of accumulated relational failures, secret sins, low self-esteem and emotional wounds from friends, co-workers and loved ones. So all-consuming is the work of carrying this baggage through life that any thought of becoming a positive change agent in the lives of others seems hopeless. *Freedom Tools* provides a way to help you 'travel light' by unpacking those bags and leaving them behind. This book will change lives—maybe even yours."

—**Rich Stearns**, president, World Vision U.S.

"This is a book that comes along only once in a generation. It brilliantly distills the complex subject of ministering to a person's innermost being into its most vital components. Using language that is simple, clear and practical, Andy Reese reveals the heart and soul of Jesus' ministry of setting captives free from bondages that are both emotion-based and sin-driven. This is ministry from the heart and by the Spirit—so simple and natural that you'll ask yourself, 'Why didn't I know this before?' *Freedom Tools* should be a required text in any program that equips the saints ⋯ ⋯ istry of the Church."

—Da⋯ ⋯ctor,
ries

"When we're born again, part of ⋯ ⋯ife of freedom and prosperity. Many ⋯ ⋯⋯s as they should because of numerous obsta⋯ ⋯⋯⋯y finds ways to implant. Do you want to know how to demolish those barriers when they appear? In this powerful book, Andy Reese gives you the *Freedom Tools* you need.

Use them and you, too, can experience the super-abundant life that God desires for you!"

—C. Peter Wagner, chancellor, Wagner Leadership Institute

"Andy Reese gives us a powerful weapon that exposes the strategies of the enemy and keys to removing his power base in many people's lives. We need more books like this to help professionally trained healers as well as laypeople who long to see the captives set free. Many have a heart for hurting people but are intimidated because they don't know *how* to really help those caught in Satan's evil web. If anyone dares to read *and* practice the how-tos of this book, the enemy will lose a lot of ground. Andy's message is clear and backed by the Word of God. And the illustrations and stories will give great understanding and revelation. This is one book you'll read and not be the same when you're done!"

—**Jill Austin**, president and founder, Master Potter Ministries; author, *Dancing with Destiny, Master Potter* and *Master Potter and the Mountain of Fire*; national and international conference speaker; www.masterpotter.com

"The mind and heart of God have been joined within the life of our dear friend and co-laborer Andy Reese. *Freedom Tools* offers piercing insights with keen discernment to empower the reader to be set free at last. This book will be a great tool for your spiritual warfare arsenal."

—**James W. and Michal Ann Goll**, co-founders, Encounters Network; authors, *Praying for Israel's Destiny, Angelic Encounters, Dream Language* and Women on the Front Lines series

"Salvation needs to reach body, soul and spirit. In order for this to happen, we often need the help of others who listen to the Holy Spirit with us, asking Him to reveal those forgotten shadowy or even darkened places of the past. Often these are childhood wounds in our soul or spirit, wounds afflicting our young hearts with no accompanying path to wholeness.

"Andy knows about those things. So do I. That's why I shout with him, 'Yes, freedom! In every part of me!' So don't just read this book; live with it and with the Holy Spirit. Gather the right people alongside you to be sure you really get free. 'It is for freedom that Christ has set us free. Stand firm, then' (Galatians 5:1, NIV)."

—**Don Finto**, author, *Your People Shall Be My People*; pastor emeritus, Belmont Church, Nashville

"*Freedom Tools* is both practical and profound. It is the right book at the right time to help bring the Church into a place of healing—spirit, soul and body. Andy Reese does a masterful job of taking a potentially complex subject and bringing it into everyone's reach. He brilliantly captures the rich truths of Scripture and presents them in a way that enables every believer to live with—and give away—this gospel of freedom."

—from the foreword by **Bill Johnson**, Bethel Church, Redding, California; author, *When Heaven Invades Earth* and *Face to Face with God*

Questions p, 86

Freedom Tools

For Overcoming Life's Tough Problems

ANDY REESE

Chosen
a division of Baker Publishing Group
Grand Rapids, Michigan

© 2008 by Andrew J. Reese

Published by Chosen Books
A division of Baker Publishing Group
P.O. Box 6287, Grand Rapids, MI 49516-6287
www.chosenbooks.com

Printed in the United States of America

Library of Congress Cataloging-in-Publication Data
Reese, Andrew.
    Freedom tools : for overcoming life's tough problems / Andy Reese.
        p.   cm.
    Includes bibliographical references and index.
    ISBN 978-0-8007-9438-5 (pbk.)
    1. Sin—Christianity. I. Title.
BV4625.R44 2008
248.8′6—dc22   2007049218

Unless otherwise indicated, Scripture is taken from the New American Standard Bible®, Copyright © 1960, 1962, 1963, 1968, 1971, 1972, 1973, 1975, 1977, 1995 by The Lockman Foundation. Used by permission.

Scripture marked NKJV is taken from the New King James Version. Copyright © 1982 by Thomas Nelson, Inc. Used by permission. All rights reserved.

Scripture marked KJV is taken from the King James Version of the Bible.

Names and some details in the stories in this book have been altered to protect the privacy of the persons involved.

11   12   13   14   15   8   7   6   5   4

In keeping with biblical principles of creation stewardship, Baker Publishing Group advocates the responsible use of our natural resources. As a member of the Green Press Initiative, our company uses recycled paper when possible. The text paper of this book is comprised of 30% post-consumer waste.

green press
INITIATIVE

To Broodje—you are my best friend
and most gentle Sozo partner ever.

Contents

Acknowledgments   9
Foreword   11
Preface   15

1. Polite Society   19

Part 1 The Ten Foundations
2. Two Foundations about God   33
3. Two Foundations about Our Enemy   47
4. Two Foundations about Us   65
5. Two Foundations about Being a First Responder   79
6. Two Foundations about Tools and Process   95

Part 2 Getting Started
7. Key Elements   107
8. Putting It Together   131

Part 3 More Advanced Tools
9. Dealing with Demons   153
10. The Four Doors   177

11. The Father Ladder   201
12. Presenting Jesus   215

Epilogue   229
Notes   241
Index   247

Acknowledgments

It is probably not a good idea to include an acknowledgments page—surely I will forget someone dear, someone we relied on. But God will not.

Sozo ministry is mostly an aggregation and organization of the revelation, insight and experience of many people—borne out of desperation to find freedom and help others find it, too. We have a few original ideas and lots of absorbed revelation. I have been privileged to cross paths with many of the pioneers and leaders in this movement.

First of all, to the Sozo team at Bethel Church, Redding, California—especially Dawna and Teresa for your guidance, mentoring, laughter and love . . . and for accepting us as comrades even though we look up to you and always will. Thank you. To Randy Clark and Fred Grewe, who sparked all of this. To Mike and Cindy Riches, who showed us an example of how it might work church-wide. To John Sandford, who has borne the heat of the day. Thank you for blessing and imparting to our team, speaking with incredible wisdom and warm humor and keeping us mesmerized with stories of the early days. We owe you a debt unpayable. To Ed Smith for organizing and focusing our conversations with Jesus. To Betsy and Chester Kylstra for communicating their detailed understanding of cause and effect in God's Kingdom. To the men and women of the Argentina revival who have tested and modeled for us God's power and His love. To Peter Horrobin for years of experience presented coherently. To Derek Prince, a spiritual mentor to many, who demonstrated for years that intellect and power are not mutually exclusive. To my fellow transplanted Minnesotan Neil Anderson, who taught us that the best defense against darkness is to know you stand in the light, and who made deliverance acceptable to almost everyone. Thank you.

To our partners in ministry, Casey and company at Belmont Church; your cheery support and love bear us up. Thank you.

To the ones who spoke strong prophetic encouragement to keep going and writing—Jill Austin, James and Michal Ann Goll, and Sandy Powell. Thank you. Thank you, Alyxius Young, who pretended she was reviewing it to learn but taught me well.

To my intercessors who pray for me and to whom belong the spoils—you are only not known on earth. And especially to the Sozo teams around the world who work tirelessly in hidden ways, keeping confidences, bearing burdens, long nights, selfless love—you vulnerable men and women of whom the world is not worthy—who know the deep satisfaction and the unabashed awe of God only comrades in spiritual arms can know. Thank you.

And to you . . . whoever you are, wherever you may be . . . for taking these bits of grace, adding yours and moving on ahead of us. We salute you. We thank you. We will meet you at the finish line!

Foreword

In the heart of every believer burns a God-born passion to see people get completely free. That freedom is promised to all in their conversion. In fact, the Greek word *sozo* means "salvation, healing and deliverance." When we do not see the full measure of *sozo* happening, we tend to change our expectations until all the good stuff of Scripture is reserved for heaven, or at least the Millennium. We end up with a powerless theology, which is a far cry from the one Jesus preached and displayed. His salvation must be experienced as He intended. Ideas (theology), no matter how profound, will never be a good replacement for the reality of a God experience.

All true ministry is really the Lord at work. But He has chosen to work through people. When these people are ill-trained and ignorant of Kingdom principles, the work is deficient and God usually gets blamed. People then form their theology around their lack of experience instead of around the true provisions of Scripture. We then tolerate bondage and unhealthy restraints in the Christian life. And what we tolerate eventually dominates.

This is not God's way. He promised life—abundant life—here and now. This promise is seen in the biblical word *freedom*. God's will for every person is the experience of freedom in every area of life. That freedom is the provision of the cross.

Many years ago Randy Clark came to Bethel Church in Redding, California, to help us progress in the move of God we were experiencing. God had been using him powerfully in healing all over the world. And while we were already experiencing wonderful miracles, we were very aware that there was so much more—and we were desperate.

But before Randy would come, he sent a friend of his to train us to help him in the ministry, so that people really would get free. So Fred Grewe came and introduced us to a more complete definition and practice of the word *sozo*.

Many of the foundational principles you see addressed in this book were first introduced to us in that week. Fred catapulted us into an irreversible journey of discovering what Jesus meant when He said, "You will know the truth, and the truth will make you free" (John 8:32).

Following Fred's training time with us, Randy came. Hundreds were healed in just a few days; but just as importantly, people were set free emotionally, mentally and spiritually. Hidden sins, secret issues of the past and unspeakable violations to individual lives all came to the surface as Randy ministered. And people got free. Really free. Marriages were healed. People always on the fringe were transformed and began to contribute to the health of the local Christian community. The training Fred provided launched us into a measure of breakthrough we had never before experienced.

Our story is the purpose of this book, yet the book is not at all about Bethel Church. Neither is it about Sozo ministry, or even the author's profound experiences and insights. It is about the normal Christian life. It is about Jesus and what He actually purchased on the cross. It is about you and me and our role in bringing about God's intended purpose for humanity.

Freedom Tools is both practical and profound. It is the right book at the right time to help bring the Church into a place of healing—spirit, soul and body. Andy Reese does a masterful job of taking a potentially complex subject and bringing it into everyone's reach. He brilliantly captures the rich truths of Scripture and presents them in a way that enables every believer to live with—and give away—this gospel of freedom.

I have great hopes for this book. It must be read and assimilated into the Christian life so that the next generation of converts will not have to learn to cover bondages and personal restraints with a theology void of experience. The theology of this book is to lead to an encounter with God, so that "where the Spirit of the Lord is, there is liberty" (2 Corinthians 3:17).

Bill Johnson
Bethel Church, Redding, California
Author, *When Heaven Invades Earth*
and *Face to Face with God*

Preface

"Woo-hoo, Mr. Reese, God answers prayer!"

Jenny's happy voice floated up to me from the beach trail far below. She and another young woman were walking arm in arm, with red eyes and sweet smiles.

I was sitting four floors above a Florida beach, working on the opening chapters of this book and playing chaperone on a high school senior trip. Only the night before I had spoken to the class about taking this last gathered opportunity to have healing conversations with their classmates, and about how to do that. These two, politely distant for two years after some blowup, believed me, and most especially, they believed God. And in a thirty-minute beach walk full of confessing, forgiving and blessing, it was gone . . . forever.

There are a lot of good home remedies out there. Some are good for the body and some for the soul. This book is about the soul kind. It is about a set of understandings and techniques—God's tools—that have been woven together into an effective approach to emotional first aid.

Beginning about a decade ago, a couple of wonderful women in Redding, California, began to organize and formulate a powerful lay approach to emotional healing and

15

spiritual restoration and freedom. Over the years many have contributed to that understanding. They decided to call it *Sozo*, a Greek word for what God does when He comes upon a hurting, lost human being and restores him or her—to save, heal and deliver from evil

Sozo.

Sozo is a very flexible tool belt on which to hang good approaches and techniques, more of which are being developed all the time.

I had been working hard on bringing the inherent simplicity of working with awesome Papa God (actually the Bible calls Him "Abba," but Papa is a good modern version of that term of affection) alive to normal people like you and me. I was wondering how I was doing. I had this idea that people could be trained to be "first responders" in the emotional-spiritual world just as in the physical one.

Then through a strange course of "chance" events, I was asked to write a book about it. I was worried that things were not ready, so I asked Papa about it. His response was similar to this email I got the same day:

> Just in case you are wondering what you are doing on the planet, after listening to you talk about what you were writing, I led my alcohol-struggling sister-in-law through the "Fruit Loop" today and God gave her two pieces of critical revelation about her past and then topped it off by filling her with a marvelous sense of His presence. She felt woozy and drunk after praying together. She's very conservative and a rare church-goer. It blew her mind! This all came out of a morning coffee discussion. What you are doing is critical! This is basic spiritual first aid/ CPR; thanks for taking the time to make it happen!

Bingo!

In this book you will learn how to be an effective first responder on a scene that seems littered with emotional and spiritual fender benders and a few wrecks; how to practice the kind of friendships that are really, really good for each other; how to be a true counterterrorist against the schemes of dark forces; and, most importantly, how to find and enjoy the warm smile and embrace of Papa God.

You will learn how to use key tools God has put in place to help bring freedom and healing to hurt and trapped people. I will start with ten key foundational understandings that frame and undergird our techniques. There is no substitute for learning to stand on and respond from the strong foundation of knowing what Christ has done for you, and knowing who, in an applied and specific way, you are in Him. Then I will give a basic framework for ministering and a simple five-step process. Finally I will describe and illustrate some more advanced tools that greatly speed up and amplify the effectiveness of the basic framework.

We are about a decade into it. And it works. Those who use these tools have grown into a network nationally and internationally. Training materials have been translated into several languages.

I hope this book encourages you to go for it, personally, in relationships and small groups, as a church and especially outside the church. There is no substitute for trying these things out for yourself and on yourself in an honest and humble way.

If you do you will find that your conversations will be forever changed, your relationships forever deepened. It will become a lifestyle, and a way of relating. You will feel "armed and dangerous" to the dark kingdom, competent to really help others. Most importantly, your awe of a living and loving Papa God will be expanded with each encounter.

And you will be hooked!

We started down this path years ago, and after seeing many people improved, healed and restored, we have no regrets . . . none.

I'm thinking you won't either.

1

Polite Society

Brethren, even if anyone is caught in any trespass, you who are spiritual, restore such a one in a spirit of gentleness; each one looking to yourself, so that you too will not be tempted. Bear one another's burdens, and thereby fulfill the law of Christ.

Galatians 6:1–2

Dear Lord, I pray that You make me into the kind of person my psychiatrist has medicated me to be.

Bumper Sticker Prayer

I do not believe in a fate that falls on men however they act. But I do believe in a fate that falls on men unless they act.

G. K. Chesterton

When the enemy comes in like a flood, the Spirit of the LORD will lift up a standard against him.

Isaiah 59:19 (NKJV)

This book is about cheating fate.

Not the kind of fate that is good and noble and exciting and glorious, but the kind that is darkly deflated, befouled by nagging moral failure, marked by a sense of harassment, emotional constraint, lonely abandonment, painful regret and gnawing hopelessness. That is the kind of fate that seems to be pandemic today—sort of a spiritual-emotional bird flu.

But there is a revolution going on. Have you noticed? It is worldwide. God is raising up a standard. Maybe it is the time of getting His Bride ready—ironing out the wrinkles, cleansing the spots.

This book is about that revolution, one that makes it possible to counter the pandemic, to steer a course toward emotional and spiritual wholeness, and to help others do so, too—your children, spouse, friends and co-workers, even strangers in chance encounters.

Polite Society

Recently a Sunday school teacher from a large church told me of an event that left him shaken and distraught. He said that he spoke to a woman after class about how he always enjoyed her husband's keen insights and thoughts about whatever was being taught, and wondered where he was that morning. She thanked him, and then in an icily quiet voice told him that that morning her husband had announced to her and the children that he was leaving them for another woman. In tears this teacher, a brilliant attorney, stated, "And what will happen is that she will just quietly slip away, another family falling through the courteous cracks of our well-mannered church. We all knew that they were in trouble. He was in a small group of men. But no one around them, myself included, knew what to say or do. We figured someone was helping. I guess no one was. It seems like no one ever is. What should I do about it, Andy? What!?"

Polite society is killing us.

We all have "stuff," and that stuff diminishes living and destroys lives. It pops up and out at the most inconvenient times. It tarnishes us and hurts those we most love. Many of us have thrown in the towel and declared stalemate over it. In this day, when the number of babies born out of wedlock is gaining on those born to two-parent families and divorces outnumber marriages, there is a need for honest, sane, wise and skilled friends. If you know how to deal with stuff, it's a seller's market.

Yet, despite this enormous and growing necessity, in most families, relationships and churches today there is almost no milieu, context or framework for recognizing and confessing sins and effectively dealing with them; for seeing wounding and having the confidence to help; for stepping into a situation and effectively bringing about healing change. We tend to hide our stuff personally, avoid it in others and quietly shun the person who wants to be vulnerable and ask for help.

When some desperate soul confesses a deep need or personal helplessness there is normally an awkward silence followed by a somewhat embarrassed and fumbling, "I'm sure it will get better," or "I'll be thinking about you." We think they really need to talk to somebody . . . somebody else. Maybe they are too fragile, and we are too clumsy. We wistfully hope they find help. We slide away, embarrassed at our own inept and weak response. We know *we* could be them tomorrow.

Maybe we *are* them, and secretly we vow to hold on another day. And we tolerate and cope, some days better than others, some people more adept at survival than others.

And should we be of a persuasion to believe in supernatural beings and admit that there just may be some spiritual involvement by, well . . . the "others" . . . you know . . . demons, then we are really in trouble. Or maybe really scared.

The wisest man ever to live, Solomon, says:

> The spirit of a man can endure his sickness, but as for a broken spirit who can bear it?
>
> Proverbs 18:14

It is our inner health that makes all the difference. With strong and healthy hearts we can withstand and contain the fallout from weakness and infirmity. We can deal with adversity and stress. But we simply cannot bear up under an inescapable internal ache, emptiness, guilt and shame. Its inexorable burden weighs us down or harries us without relief.

We cannot stand it.

Yet, we as "laypeople" feel mostly inadequate to say or do much of anything, even when invited. Most of what we know about helping hurting people we saw on afternoon talk shows or evening reality-based displays of human misery and stupidity. We are intimidated by people's problems and so want to consign them to the overwhelmed professional ministerial and counseling system. It has to get very bad to actually go for help. And so it *does* get very bad.

This situation is not God's plan. It is not "abundant life."

He tells us to confess our sins one to another and pray for one another that we might be healed. He urges us to gently reprove and restore when we see one overtaken in sin, and to bind up the brokenhearted. He says that bringing dark things to the light is the only way to walk in true communion. He says our path will grow brighter and brighter, from glory to glory.[1]

God calls us to the place where we, as individuals, can partner with Him and each other in dealing with the pervasive sin and wounding around and within us. He desires that we not leave each other in a place of "tolerable desperation," coping with tormenting internal issues or dull emotional aches, and call it good enough.

We are all in this together. Together with each other. Together with God.

But how?

God has a plan. It is unfolding. He is behind it. He is actively bringing it about in the earth today. I've experienced it. Thousands of others have, too.

Keep reading.

First Aid

Humans can seem so complex. To be helpful appears to be a daunting task.

I took yet another cruise through the official psychiatric diagnostic book the other day (*Diagnostic and Statistical Manual of Mental Disorders IV*), and felt myself stepping into a parallel universe of techno-talk and multiplied treatment modalities. Complex and arcane language dominates—and perhaps *must* dominate—for mental health professionals to communicate with exactitude. It is certainly intimidating. Is *everything* a disease, a syndrome or a disorder? Does everything require multiple counseling sessions or mood-altering drugs?

Emotional needs are, in many ways, like medical needs. Ninety percent of the need is satisfied by home-based, lay-administered first aid and over-the-counter medicine. It is seldom cancer, it rarely requires open-heart surgery and it is usually not life threatening. And when it *is* life threatening would you not be glad some friend caught it early enough and with enough insight to refer you to professional help?

It takes eight years plus to be a competent physician. But it takes only a few hours to learn basic CPR; only a day to learn first aid basics—bleeding, breathing, heartbeat.

A Band-Aid is *just* what we need if the problem is a cut.

Much of what we encounter in people are just emotional scratches, relational burns, behavioral headaches, minor dark infections, sprained morals or stubbed egos. Most of us are not a millimeter from meltdown or an inch from insanity. And when it is more than that? We can help spot it and learn where to refer. That is a valuable and good thing, too.

In the real world, we are in desperate need for first responders, those trained in basic first aid for the soul. That is why I so love the lifestyle, the "way" that this book is about. With simple instruction and a little practice, we find we *are* competent to help another find relief and freedom. I do not have to be an emotional open-heart surgeon. Most people do not need that.

The Sozo First Aid Model

It is the responsibility, and within the latent capability, of every believer to be competent to help and encourage friends and family—to be able to perform first aid for the soul, to be the first line of defense against darkness. Paul says it best:

> And concerning you, my brethren, I myself also am convinced that you yourselves are full of goodness, filled with all knowledge and able also to admonish one another.
>
> Romans 15:14

That is the idea: brethren (that is, people in relationship), full of and motivated by goodness and love, holding the right tools, empowered and led by God, able to gently admonish, encourage and help set free.

The Bible refers to that process, that gift, that thing God is doing to bring about internal healing and freedom by a single Greek word: *sōzō*. It means "to save, heal and deliver." It is all one package, one and the same Greek word.[2] So that is what we call it, too.

Jesus came to "sozo" us.

Over the last ten years, thousands have found increased peace and freedom, and experienced the freshness of encounters with a loving, living God. Many are learning how to walk out the scriptural injunctions to complete each other, to care for, encourage and even reprove each other. Some encounters are very dramatic, some gentle and peaceful. All occur in an informal, confidential, honoring, one-on-one or small-group setting, friend with friend.

This is not counseling—that is properly the purview of trained professionals, not first responders. This is about a couple of friends going together to God to get help in time of need.

In a nutshell, Sozo is a God-led framework helping to free individuals from the effects of wounding and sin, and delivering people from the snares and presence of the demonic. It is done in overt partnership with God through finding past and present believed lies and points of access and removing or changing them; establishing healing, blessing and obedience in their place; and restoring individuals to relationship with Papa God and a more fruitful and fulfilling walk.

In Sozo, we depend on God on a moment-by-moment basis. We like to say, "If God does not show up, we cannot fake Sozo ministry!" That is unusual, I think.

Sozo is a changing and growing "lay" approach to working with God in setting each other free. There is no single training manual, proponent church or ministry or certification process. It is more like Alcoholics Anonymous and less like

"Sozo, Inc." It makes the best use of tools and approaches developed by others and modified for our use and to fit our DNA. No minister is a "professional"—though many have had years of training and experience in Christian ministry. Some are psychiatrists, some are certified counselors who use the tools on a daily basis, and most, like me, are just compassionate knuckleheads.

So you can fit in just fine.

Bob, Belief, Brain, Behavior

So . . . is it wacko? Is it spiritual mumbo jumbo?

Let's look at our friend Bob's car.

The right way to start a car, as intended by its "creator," is with a starter. Failing in that, we can always try to jump-start it. Failing in that, and if it is a stick shift, we can always push-start it. And if that does not work, we can take it to a mechanic, figuring something is broken.

Let's look at Bob.

Bob is feeling down. You and he are having coffee and he expresses dispirited feelings, sad moods and poor behaviors. You are wondering what to do and how to think about your friend Bob. He is like that car that will not start.

If we try to get Bob help we may find some professional who will recommend changes to his environment, behavior, relational skills, cognitive reasoning structures or brain chemistry. Lots of ways to start the car—none wrong if they work.

That's great, but what can *we* do about it?

I am a spirit being, I have a soul and I live in a body.[3] The Bible is pretty clear about this. Our Creator intends for us to live from the inside out. What we believe in our hearts drives all else (see figure 1).[4] The *beliefs* in our hearts are like a car starter—they are intended to propel our lives. God intends our hearts to be powered from within—from communion with Him within our spirits.

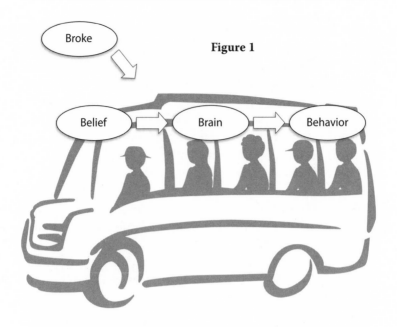

Figure 1

Beliefs then influence the thoughts and operation of our *brains*. Our brains are meant to be structured over time through the flow of sound truth and gentle love. We are to automatically and effortlessly think along peaceful and healthy mental pathways—as brain scientists say, "Neurons that fire together wire together." The proper wiring and functioning of the brain then guides and directs *behavior*. And through proper maintenance and protection, we do not break down emotionally or behaviorally. We are not *broken*.

Our approach, and the subject of this book, is to work mostly from the inside out on *beliefs* and also on spiritually *broken* aspects of lives (the result of negative spiritual events). We think that when Jesus said, "You will know the truth, and the truth will make you free,"[5] He meant it in a very practical and applied way. We may advise people with unexplained issues to get a thorough physical to make sure there is not a true physical *brain* malfunction, and we may give advice on right thinking and on responsible *behavior*.

We take this approach first because experience in thousands of settings shows it can be very effective, and at worst it is still encouraging and loving when applied within our framework. Second, it is well framed within the truth found in Scripture. And third, we take this approach because we can. It is simple to learn, powerful in application, low pressure, informal and well within the definition of "first aid." It is within the reach of most people.

I have talked with medical and counseling professionals, some of whom use this approach in both practice and in their daily lives, who have stated that some of the results they have witnessed from this kind of ministry are amazing, effective and often scientifically unexplainable. Most, when they understand what we are about, are not opposed to it even if it does not fit their particular model of human change.

To be sure, some smile with benign tolerance, some even frown. To be truthful, sometimes a ministry session can be lovingly and gently *ineffective* at bringing about lasting change. But even so, the person feels loved, listened to and prayed for. And that's not bad!

Book Objectives and Organization

The objectives of this book are to give a sound basis and clear understanding for giving spiritual first aid, and to make you familiar with various tools and techniques.

My goal is to *impart* to you an expectation that God will use you both to set others free and to pass on what you are learning.

The book is organized into:

- *Ten Foundations* (part 1)—The ten key foundations are our DNA, how we think about helping each other. Do not skip them. Having the foundations without

28

mastering the tools will still work. Having the tools without the foundations is disastrous.

- *Getting Started* (part 2)—We combine a simple five-phase process, "the fruit loop," with five different kinds of issues we face ("WESUD"). It helps keep us on track and chasing only fat rabbits. You can minister with just these steps and basic core techniques. It is a good place to start.

- *More Advanced Tools* (part 3)—We have borrowed, modified and even developed some tools as powerful shortcuts to quickly get at the key issues of WESUD.

Obligatory Disclaimer

I understand that this book will raise as many questions as it answers. As I stated earlier, humans can be very complex. But it seems God often deals simply and wisely with that complexity. This book is not a treatise designed to convince anyone. It is a brief instruction book put together because of the great need out there for a first line of defense against demonic intrusion, pain, entanglement, lies and sin. I do not try, in this book, to answer every question and objection raised about its foundations, root doctrines and use of the tools—though those answers do exist.

It is a good start.

Sozo does not train or certify anyone. It is simply a set of commonly shared understandings. Each person must use their own wisdom and discretion and remember that they should (and in some cases *must*) get help with such things as child abuse, domestic violence, suicide, true mental illness, dissociation and extreme demonic control.[6] This is not to frighten you away but to let you know that you may encounter things that you should refer to others—you probably already have, just by being alive and human.

Only yesterday I stood hugging a young man good-bye. He had flown in from the West Coast to meet with a couple of us. His eyes were red, his face alight. "I *never* felt this peaceful in all my life. I'm not sure why but this is sooo cool!" We all wanted to bottle it. We sent him on his way with a bit of homework and encouragement. What a great day! He emailed weeks later to say it was "still working," just like that battery-powered bunny.

PART 1

The Ten Foundations

2

Two Foundations about God

The devil is a better theologian than any of us but is a devil still.

A. W. Tozer

I am afraid that, as the serpent deceived Eve by his craftiness, your minds will be led astray from the simplicity and purity of devotion to Christ.

2 Corinthians 11:3

Sacred cows make the best hamburger.

Mark Twain

Betsy looked very small sitting on our living room couch. She's 22. But tonight she was eight all over again—and all, all alone.

"I'm sorry I'm falling apart. I needed someone to talk to. I hate to take up your evening. Is that okay?" she cries.

"Sure, sweetie bear, you are worth a thousand nights!" My wife holds her. We wait. We sense Papa God gently enter the room. It is time.

She shared; we listened. Betsy's mother had died of cancer, a cruel and untimely death, years earlier. Betsy was bereft, abandoned, cast adrift. To comfort her, I suppose, she was told, "I guess God needed your mom more than you did." *Not possible*, she thought. *How can that be? No! Yes? Oh no. . . .* She whimpered, struck momentarily senseless. It was the only explanation offered. It sounded logical, true and even believable. After all, an adult said it.

On the inside, the voice that hissed to Eve in the Garden whispered once again to the naïve eight-year-old in the first-person singular, *I cannot trust God; He is not safe. He's unknowable and unapproachable.* The old, old story written again on a tender and trusting human heart. She swallowed numbing pain—who can question *God*? And on the inside the confusion seeped in, walls went up. *Never again will I trust this God.*

She cried. We cried, too.

There is more to her story, and our conversation, of course, and we will revisit Betsy later . . . and some others. Maybe your story will be told, too. But in the end, after gentle Jesus had spoken powerfully to her and she was peaceful, and the Kleenex box was empty, I asked her a simple question: "Betsy, what would it mean if God was not the one who took your mother? What would it mean if Papa God grieved with you, if He hurt, too?"

She paused, as if deep inner places were being polled for input. And I'll never forget her answer:

"It would mean . . . it would mean . . . *everything.*"

The Problem of Pain and Blame

The plane crashed on takeoff. Wrong runway. Everyone was killed but the co-pilot. He exclaimed from his hospital bed to a news reporter, "Why would God do this to me?" His mother answered, "Honey, it wasn't God. It just happened. That's all."

That scenario plays out all the time, everywhere: "Why would God?" versus "Maybe God didn't." There is a battle raging for the hearts of men—and it focuses right here. Why are things the way they are? Why do bad things happen? Why is there evil? What is God's role and, by implication, who is God . . . really?

There are *no* easy answers. None.

But when we look around it seems like something strange is going on. Someone is getting framed. Today, among God's children, many have come to think that perhaps God may be the ultimate author of sickness, torment and destruction and that His purpose may be to "teach us a lesson," or to "build character" or to "bring about a mysterious ultimate good."

He takes away young mothers to teach eight-year-olds lessons.

"Okay," we say, "if He is not the triggerman of torment, then He is the acquiescing force behind the triggerman— uninterested, uninvolved, busy with China." He hung an "Out to Lunch" sign on the universe and went . . . away. His mysterious ways are higher than ours and not to be questioned. We will understand one day.

Looking over my experience with hundreds of people, I find that this thought process often produces a result that builds a wall between an empty, confused or aching human being and the only source of help he or she desperately needs. For Betsy, the thinking went something like this: *Since I never know when I will get an open hand or a backhand from God, I will keep my distance from this mysterious and capricious God. I'll keep my mouth shut and hide.* A crust forms around the heart that knows it badly needs daddy and that God is certainly not he.

This "mysterious God" dynamic may be an understandable inference from prayers that are not answered and ministry that appears to be of no avail. It may be the natural deduction of a child who has experienced neither the warmth of a loving earthly father, nor the truth of a loving Abba.

It is easy to accept theoretical theological explanations of evil if there is "insufficient appreciation for the radicality of evil in the world."[1] But when looking into children's faces and seeing the horrific scars of these innocent victims of evil, it is much harder to explain things away in terms of a God who is in control but mysterious. When we have to ascribe to God such horrors, cruelty and demonic insanity, the two ideas then do not sit so comfortably in our hearts and consciousness. If God were to be tried in a court of law, and the things attributed to Him were the testimony, He would be locked away forever . . . even given the death penalty. Maybe crucified.

What would it mean if that reasoning were flawed—fatally?

Maybe everything.

A Different Understanding

We live with a very simple, maybe naïve, understanding well articulated by a pastor friend named Bill Johnson. It is our first and most important foundation:

FOUNDATION #1—

1. God is good. Satan is bad.
2. Your freedom is God's will.
3. We have hidden enemies.
4. Issues are not random.
5. There is always a reason.
6. Prisoners and captives.
7. Partners with God.
8. A culture of honor.
9. Apply God's solutions.
10. An event and a process.

God is good. Satan is bad.

It seems, at least in my reading, that the early Church, those closest to the source, did not have the same debate and confusion about sickness, sin and torment that modern man has developed. The question of "why do bad things happen to good people?" never seemed to be one of hot theological debate. They saw they were at

36

Early church

war. Sometimes there were casualties . . . even eternal ones. They prayed when people were sick . . . and often saw healing. They believed in, encountered and cast out demons . . . and sometimes still did not get everything settled. But they expected demons to flee.

They confessed and forgave, healed the brokenhearted, comforted the afflicted and did all they knew to bring people to a place of health and wholeness—even if some did not fully receive it at that instant, or ever. It was not intellectually complex or confusing. Other things may have been in flux and formation, but not that. The enemy was clear. It was a battle, a war—with victory for the good guys clearly anticipated. They seemed to understand that it was possible to *know* God even when you cannot fully *explain* Him. And they turned the world upside down.[2]

Could it be that some things happen that are patently *not* God's will? This is potentially disturbing to some. But when you read a Scripture such as 2 Peter 3:9, you are drawn to this conclusion. And a warfare theology begins to make sense.

> The Lord is not slow about His promise, as some count slowness, but is patient toward you, not wishing for any to perish but for all to come to repentance.
>
> 2 Peter 3:9

Some clearly do perish. And according to this Scripture it is not God's will that they do so. And it seems equally clear, by implication, that the string of events and happenings that lead to that perishing must also not be God's will. Yet it happens. We are at war—often with ourselves.

Free Will, Dark Enemies

The late William Sloan Coffin, social activist and chaplain of Yale University, in an interview with Terry Gross of the radio program *Fresh Air*, said this when speaking about the death of his own son in a tragic car accident:[3]

> People have some very goofy ideas about how the will of God operates—"I guess it was the will of God . . . "—as if it is the will of God that anybody gets blown up, that anybody gets shot. God was not behind the wheel—my son was. God's heart was the first of all hearts to break. God was not in the event. He was in the response to the event.
>
> What is hard for people is that we really do have free will. You have to have freedom if love is to be the name of the game. And if we have free will we are free to do both good and bad things—free to kill, free to love. To blame God for what people do with their freedom is not fair except in the same way that you would blame an adult if you saw a child smash an expensive watch. It is your fault for giving the child the watch in the first place. Now you can blame God for giving us human freedom. Maybe we're not ready for it, maybe we can't handle it.

We have free will. God does not violate that will. He does not want robots. He respects us too much to dominate us. Though He knows man is made to walk in relationship, not independence, He lets us choose.

And we have a dark enemy who hates God and us.

In a warfare worldview we expect bad things to happen to good people, maybe *especially* to good people. We anticipate that "in the world you will have tribulation."[4] The warfare understanding means that we accept the idea that there are angels and demons, that they are real, autonomous agents and that they impact human affairs for better or worse. They, too, have free will, and some, unprovoked, chose to rebel.

Humans, devils, God and angels. This can cause some confusion.

For example, we often hear, at the tail end of some terrible ordeal, sickness or suffering, that the person feels stronger, knows God better, had a change of heart about something important, etc. And we think to ourselves, *See what good thing came out of this. It must have been from God.* And we are confused. We mistake outcome for origin. Because the outcome is good we think the origin is, too. And so we distort God. Maybe the outcome is good because God comes to the rescue of His children.

He is a better chess player than Satan.

We wish there were easy answers to each and every situation. We believe there *are* answers in every situation, and increasingly we come to understand them. I remember spending time with a young woman who had been horribly abused. I asked her where God was when it happened and she was quite emphatic about two things: the abuser had free will and used it to abuse her, and in some way God limited his right, protected her (in this case through dissociation) and provided both grace and strength for her to endure it, escape some of it and recover stronger than ever in the end.

She understood what many do not: We children of Adam made a choice long ago, a choice to follow the evil one and give authority over this world to him.[5] It is an evil age, and we are still paying on that note.

I think there is one simple way to gain right focus—watch Jesus.

Jesus Is the Last Word

Jesus is the best picture of God ever taken. Hebrews makes it very clear:

> God, after He spoke long ago to the fathers in the prophets in many portions and in many ways, in these last days has spoken to us in His Son. . . . He is the radiance of His glory and the exact representation of His nature.
>
> Hebrews 1:1–3

Jesus Himself says:

> He who has seen Me has seen the Father.
>
> John 14:9

We should question anything we think we know about God that cannot be observed in the ways and words of Jesus.

Jesus is God's best, highest, consummate and most accurate expression of the essence of God's character. God's purposes, His gentle yet firm ways among needy men and women, are to be observed in Jesus. Jesus' reaction to demonic intrusion is an exact representation of His Father's. Jesus' response to those caught shamefully in sin is precisely His Father's. The ways of Jesus among brokenhearted men and women unerringly express His Father's heart. His attitude and action toward disease accurately reflect His Father's. His reaction to hypocritical religiosity, to burdening men with rules and false teaching and to moneychangers in the temple, exactly mirrors His Father's intense anger.

And Jesus makes this one thing *very* clear, *very* simple:

> The thief comes only to steal and kill and destroy; I came that they may have life, and have it abundantly.
>
> John 10:10

Seems simple enough.

It is not God if it clearly looks and smells like stealing, killing or destroying. It is probably God if it looks and feels like life—lavish, abundant and free.

So what was that like? What did it feel like? Look like?

When we look at Jesus we never once see Him attributing to God untimely death, demonic oppression, hardship, human torment, misery, torture, murder or sin. We never see Him explaining things through some convoluted logic about sovereignty. He constantly portrays the Father as good and welcoming, even partying after regaining the lost coin, lost sheep and the Prodigal Son.[6]

We see Him conquering, forgiving, removing, healing, comforting and confronting. He is filled with compassion, moved with compassion, overflowing with compassion. We see Him engaging evil—demonic and human. He cut short every funeral He attended—because in the world people die outside of the will of the Father. That is what the Father's heart is . . . exactly.

And we should take it very personally.

What about You?

We may agree that God is good and at work to heal the world. But when the eyes of the Lord turn to us we may tend to shy away. We may feel like some internal issue is hopeless, is "just the way I am" or is "my cross to bear." We may feel like we will never be able to get past some unbearable wound. Like a bad back or trick knee, we learn to live with it.

That is a big fat lie!

Jesus came for two main purposes:

> You know that He appeared in order to take away sins. . . .
> The Son of God appeared for this purpose, to destroy the
> works of the devil.
>
> 1 John 3:5, 8

Regardless of your life circumstances, know this: Freedom is God's will—*your* freedom specifically is God's will.[7] That is our second foundation.

<table>
<tr><td>1. God is good. Satan is bad.</td></tr>
<tr><td>2. Your freedom is God's will.</td></tr>
<tr><td>3. We have hidden enemies.</td></tr>
<tr><td>4. Issues are not random.</td></tr>
<tr><td>5. There is always a reason.</td></tr>
<tr><td>6. Prisoners and captives.</td></tr>
<tr><td>7. Partners with God.</td></tr>
<tr><td>8. A culture of honor.</td></tr>
<tr><td>9. Apply God's solutions.</td></tr>
<tr><td>10. An event and a process.</td></tr>
</table>

FOUNDATION #2—

Your freedom is God's will.

Everything in your life that is not part of God's destiny for you is fair game for removal.

The same death on the cross that purchased our sin purchased our freedom.[8] We can be very sure that when we are about doing the two things in the verses from 1 John above, we are moving directly in line with God's clearly stated will.

The truth is, I am predestined to be conformed to the image of Jesus.[9] Predestined. He began, and will complete, the good work in me.[10] He authored and will perfect.[11] He works to will and do inside me.[12] It is a done deal in His eyes. He completed the work of your freedom when He died and was resurrected, and now you are God's child, His type, His possession. And His is the only opinion that counts!

A friend once told me, "God has this unreasonable and consistent habit of coming to us from our destiny, not our history." God sees the finished product and is not at all discouraged. He can call Gideon a "valiant warrior" even while he is hiding in a threshing mill.[13] He can call Saul to be Paul even in the midst of his persecution of this new sect called The Way.[14] He chooses knuckleheads to be His beloved sons and daughters, and for greatness.

Maybe He has no better option.

Close Your Eyes

You, the one whose hairs are all numbered.[15] The one whose thoughts are all known before you even think them and whose life was carefully considered before your birth.[16] The one whom the Father thinks about more times each day than there are grains of sand on the seashore.[17]

That one.

You . . . are His favorite.

He wants to spoil you.

I wish right now I could have you close your eyes and just listen. Maybe you can do that and still read. Everything you are about to read is straight from Scripture, straight from the heart of Papa God. It is a brief enumeration of the overwhelming evidence of Papa God's love for you. "How do I love thee?" He says. "Let me count the ways." It is His love letter to you.[18] If you imagine God the Father as distant, angry, even abusive, let Him change your mind about His goodness. Let Him convince you.

My Child . . .

You may not know me, but I know everything about you. Psalm 139:1

I know when you sit down and when you rise up. Psalm 139:2

I am familiar with all your ways. Psalm 139:3

Even the very hairs on your head are numbered. Matthew 10:29–31

For you were made in my image. Genesis 1:27

In me you live and move and have your being. Acts 17:28

For you are my offspring. Acts 17:28

I knew you even before you were conceived. Jeremiah 1:4–5

I chose you when I planned creation. Ephesians 1:11–12

You were not a mistake, for all your days are written in my book. Psalm 139:15–16

I determined the exact time of your birth and where you would live. Acts 17:26

You are fearfully and wonderfully made. Psalm 139:14

I knit you together in your mother's womb. Psalm 139:13

*And brought you forth on the day
you were born. Psalm 71:6*

*I have been misrepresented by those
who don't know me. John 8:41–44*

*I am not distant and angry, but am the
complete expression of love. 1 John 4:16*

*And it is my desire to lavish my
love on you. 1 John 3:1*

*Simply because you are my child and
I am your Father. 1 John 3:1*

*I offer you more than your earthly
father ever could. Matthew 7:11*

For I am the perfect Father. Matthew 5:48

*Every good gift that you receive comes
from my hand. James 1:17*

*For I am your provider and I meet all
your needs. Matthew 6:31–33*

*My plan for your future has always been
filled with hope. Jeremiah 29:11*

*Because I love you with an
everlasting love. Jeremiah 31:3*

*My thoughts toward you are countless as the
sand on the seashore. Psalm 139:17–18*

*And I rejoice over you with
singing. Zephaniah 3:17*

I will never stop doing good to you. Jeremiah 32:40

For you are my treasured possession. Exodus 19:5

*I desire to establish you with all my heart
and all my soul. Jeremiah 32:41*

44

*And I want to show you great and
marvelous things. Jeremiah 33:3*

*If you seek me with all your heart, you
will find me. Deuteronomy 4:29*

*Delight in me and I will give you the
desires of your heart. Psalm 37:4*

*For it is I who gave you those
desires. Philippians 2:13*

*I am able to do more for you than you
could possibly imagine. Ephesians 3:20*

*For I am your greatest encourager.
2 Thessalonians 2:16–17*

*I am also the Father who comforts you in
all your troubles. 2 Corinthians 1:3–4*

*When you are brokenhearted, I am
close to you. Psalm 34:18*

*As a shepherd carries a lamb, I have carried
you close to my heart. Isaiah 40:11*

*One day I will wipe away every tear
from your eyes. Revelation 21:3–4*

*And I'll take away all the pain you have
suffered on this earth. Revelation 21:3–4*

*I am your Father, and I love you even
as I love my Son, Jesus. John 17:23*

For in Jesus, my love for you is revealed. John 17:26

*He is the exact representation of
my being. Hebrews 1:3*

*He came to demonstrate that I am for
you, not against you. Romans 8:31*

And to tell you that I am not counting your sins. 2 Corinthians 5:18–19

Jesus died so that you and I could be reconciled. 2 Corinthians 5:18–19

His death was the ultimate expression of my love for you. 1 John 4:10

I gave up everything I loved that I might gain your love. Romans 8:31–32

If you receive the gift of my Son, Jesus, you receive me. 1 John 2:23

And nothing will ever separate you from my love again. Romans 8:38–39

Come home and I'll throw the biggest party heaven has ever seen. Luke 15:7

I have always been Father, and will always be Father. Ephesians 3:14–15

I am waiting for you. Luke 15:11–32

Love, Your Dad, Almighty God

3

Two Foundations about Our Enemy

No wonder, for even Satan disguises himself as an angel of light.

2 Corinthians 11:14

There is nothing more exhilarating than to be shot at without result.

Winston Churchill

Every journey has a secret destination of which the traveler is unaware.

Martin Buber

Recognizing Evil around Us

It was all hush and mahogany.

I was efficiently ushered into the presence of the pastor of a very large and important church.

I was all jitters and politeness.

All my human moral support had called and canceled fifteen minutes earlier. I sometimes hate not being controlling anymore!

He was a gray-haired, quietly imposing, wizened man, the head of a great religious corporation. He had years and years of ministerial experience on me, that was for sure. He smiled warmly and I liked him immediately, but that did not keep my hands from shaking just a little. He came around his large desk and led me to ornate couches in a sitting area.

He had heard of something called "Sozo" a few weeks earlier when the daughter of one of his elders experienced a miraculous turnaround from "suicidal and depressed" to "glowing and happy" seemingly overnight. It was an unusually amazing transformation even for those of us who feel like "amazing" is a steady diet. He wanted to see and question someone about what had happened, and by process of elimination—or desertion—I was selected.

"Now I know that demons are in the Bible so they are real," he said, "you don't have to convince me of that. But that girl was a real exception. We don't have many like that in our church."

This is when I pray that deeply theological ministry prayer, "Help, God!" And then a thought came. . . .

There is an interesting verse in the gospel of Mark about Jesus. Like a lot of scriptural passages, it doesn't seem strange or thought provoking until you close your eyes and really think it through.

And He went into their synagogues throughout all Galilee, preaching and casting out the demons.

Mark 1:39

So here it is: Saturday night at your friendly neighborhood synagogue. The men are sitting around reciting Torah . . . and He is casting out demons.

Now my campfire-horror-story-based idea of this picture would be one with dark scary music, a spooky room full of sinister-looking people floating about in a Fu Manchu–bearded threatening manner, with twisting heads, chilling shrieks and green slime. Synagogue must have been something else.

But that is not the way it was at all.

Who were these people? Was the synagogue filled with screaming, frothing people chasing each other with knives and bad masks? Hardly. They were just normal people . . . farmers, shepherds, carpenters, housewives, traders, weavers . . . just Eli, Seth, Mary and Josiah types. They would be considered "normal" moral church people in any society. Yet they were somehow under the influence of demons.

And today?

They are the guys next door and our cousins. They are our brothers-in-law . . . and they are us—stock traders, small business owners, factory workers, insurance salesmen, housewives, store clerks, carpenters, engineers—Kip, Henry, Susan and Ralph types. Yet . . .

Jesus and His disciples dealt with demons as a matter of course. We have it on the authority of all early writers who refer to the subject at all that in the first centuries all Christians were able by the power of Christ to deliver demoniacs (or *energumens*), and their success was appealed to by the early apologists as a strong argument for the divine origin of Christianity. For example, church father Tertullian (A.D. 155–230) illustrates the early Church's prevailing conviction and practice. Speaking of demons masquerading as gods, he addresses the pagans of his time:

> Let a person be brought before your tribunals who is plainly under demoniacal possession. The wicked spirit, bidden speak by the followers of Christ, will as readily make the

truthful confession that he is a demon as elsewhere he has falsely asserted that he is a god.[1]

Was Jesus just ignorant or unaware that this was purely a psychological phenomenon? Was He just pandering to the primitive people of His time?

Careful.

This is a touchy subject. The first question we are always asked is, "So, is the movie *The Exorcist* true?" Which we ignore. But the second question is the telling one. "Can someone (or 'I') really be 'demon possessed'?"

Much of the Christian confusion in answering "the question" stems from an unfortunate translation in the King James, where some were said to be "possessed" by a demon. "So," the argument goes, "if I belong to Christ, then how can I be possessed by another?" The Greek word translated "possessed," as numerous better spoken authors have explained, is either *daimonizomai*, which carries a meaning of "demonized" without the ownership overtone, or *echo*, meaning several different things, notably "with, accompanied by, or gripped by." So we can be influenced without being owned, nudged without being overwhelmed, controlled without knowing it.

It may even feel just like . . . well, like us—only maybe us on a bad day on steroids.

So let us keep that one in mind: "influenced without being owned." Maybe I just rent out a room or grant an easement.

Demonic Influence

Back to the story line.

"Well, Dr. Harold," I said, with some growing inkling of inspiration, "look at this verse:

The Lord's bond-servant must not be quarrelsome, but be kind to all, able to teach, patient when wronged, with gentleness correcting those who are in opposition, if perhaps God may grant them repentance leading to the knowledge of the truth, and they may come to their senses and escape from the snare of the devil, having been held captive by him to do his will.

2 Timothy 2:24–26

"How would a person look to you, this one who Scripture says has been held captive by the devil to do his will?" He read the verse in context, pondered a minute, then looked me straight in the eye with a smile playing around the corners of his mouth. "*That* would be my elder board!" He then quickly indicated that he was officially kidding.

So this Scripture, written to a young pastor about the kind of people he would encounter in his church, says that sometimes when he encountered someone who was unusually and uncontrollably divisive, argumentative, critical, blind to their own faults or opinionated, it might not be just them. There may be a sort of puppet master at work behind the scenes. This Scripture indicates that it may be, at least partially, demonic in origin.

If we are Bible readers or Sunday school goers, we may be familiar with the more extreme biblical examples of demons showing up and being cast out: Legion and the madman, the epileptic boy and the spirit of divination.[2] But Scripture abounds with less obvious examples of demonic influence and partial control, and in almost every case it is written to Christians describing a "Christian" phenomenon.

Imagine how Peter the one-time fisherman must have felt when *he* was in this situation—on the receiving end. He has just called Jesus "the Messiah," and he receives the highest praise and promise of all time: "I will build My Church on *this* rock." So, maybe figuring he is *the man*, he continues to direct Jesus, telling Him He certainly cannot now go and die: "What about that church we are going to build?" Jesus looks and speaks right through him to the puppet master: "Get thee behind me, Satan."[3] Jesus called it what it was.

One of my favorites, sure to cause fidgeting among Bible majors, is this:

> But the Spirit explicitly says that in later times some will fall away from the faith, paying attention to deceitful spirits and doctrines of demons.
>
> 1 Timothy 4:1

What might a "doctrine of demons" look like? Have you encountered one? Are they always obvious, dark and cultic? I am not sure. They were not always easy to distinguish in Paul's time.

Pondering? Here's one more, though Scripture is full of additional examples:[4]

> Be angry, and yet do not sin; do not let the sun go down on your anger, and do not give the devil an opportunity.
>
> Ephesians 4:26–27

The word *opportunity* is the Greek work *topos*, from which we get *topography*. It means lost ground or territory within us. How might a person appear who *has* let the sun go down on his or her anger, raging inside against a harsh and critical father, every night for a decade? We might experience them as sarcastic, wounded, angry, bitter, withdrawn, biting or sour. They have lost control of territory within themselves. And God says it is, in part, demonic in origin.

Like the Jews in the synagogue long ago, unless it is an obvious out-of-control manifestation, we almost never attribute what is happening to the demonic realm. And it almost *never* is obvious. That is the first foundation about the dark side, and our third foundation overall.

FOUNDATION #3—

We have hidden enemies.

1. God is good. Satan is bad.
2. Your freedom is God's will.
3. We have hidden enemies.
4. Issues are not random.
5. There is always a reason.
6. Prisoners and captives.
7. Partners with God.
8. A culture of honor.
9. Apply God's solutions.
10. An event and a process.

Dr. Harold broke in, "That would be half my church [smile]. Okay, you've got me on the bus. Now, what do you suggest we should do about it here in our church? How would you introduce these ideas?"

I opened my mouth for my standard spiel—then—long pause. We both stared out the window at the lineup of Mercedes-Benzes and BMWs in the parking lot. Were these soccer moms and their children harassed by demons? Did they know it? Was that idea even remotely within the realm of consideration? He looked at me with a weary smile and said, "Our county, those people out there, has the highest per capita income and also the highest divorce rate in the state. Says something, doesn't it? But how do we turn the Queen Mary . . . hmmm?" We stared some more. It's not easy bucking the system . . . even when it's killing us.

We will discuss more about our dark enemies in chapter 9, but first let us expose an amazing thing about our lives, and ground zero of this dark world: our next foundation.

Wheel of Misfortune?

Christ said, "In the world you will have tribulation."[5] The word for *tribulation* means "stress." You will *have* stress. It was a promise. You will have pressure, strain, anxiety, tension and hassle in your life. No exemptions. When you are going the right direction, you will meet the enemy head-on. Those meetings are not random. They have a specific diabolical purpose. Let me illustrate.

It made no sense, of course.

When Dave, my first aid ministry partner that day, and I first met Ben an hour earlier, I had gotten a fleeting impression on my inner screen of some old Vincent van Gogh painting; you know, the one with his ear bandaged and all the bright swirling colors. *How absurd is that? Andy, you need to concentrate, this kid is looking to you for help. . . . Focus, focus, focus.*

We had worked through a few issues in Ben's life: some sexual failings, some old soul ties. Tears were shed. Forgiveness was spoken. Real relief came when he finally unburdened himself and felt God's forgiveness. Some new freedom was gained. Great! Find the doors, close the doors, do Kingdom business.

Some days, forgiveness *is* the issue. Some days, confessed sin *is* the focus.

But not this day.

In my gut I felt we were not at the core. We were clearing away branches. There was something deeper hidden just below our senses, but what? My heart pounded a little, a sure sign of impending vulnerability on my part.

When I am weak, He is strong. When I am dead, He is invincible.

I know Papa God elbowed some angel in heaven's throne room and said, "Think I can't use a knucklehead? Watch this!"

You always find the fruit out on a limb . . . where it feels a little unsafe.

So I said it: "This is probably a silly question, but does 'van Gogh' mean anything to you?"

A smile crept into the corners of Dave's mouth. He's always up for an adventure. Ben's eyes widened in surprise, then with a bad poker face, he said, "Why would you ask that?"

"Well, the picture with his ear bandaged popped into my mind earlier, but really, I have no clue." No sense being dishonest—I didn't have a clue. And to pretend otherwise is the surest way to failure, nicely robed in religion.

God's presence seemed to slip quietly into the room. A long silent moment, a quivering lip, quickly averted eyes, arms wrapped around a suddenly painful heart. Then a tear slowly slipped down his cheek and into his scraggly beard.

My partner passed me a quick note. "*Bingo!*" was all it said. Very funny . . . just what I needed. I began to probe with gentle questions, on spiritual tiptoes, one ear on the inner flow of God, one on Ben's answers.

"Funny . . . I just pasted a picture by van Gogh into my journal yesterday. I don't know why," Ben wondered. "In fact, last summer I drove to Washington, D.C., and slept in my car to attend a van Gogh exhibit. It sort of scares me. Strange you should ask about that . . . way strange."

"What exactly scares you?" "Jesus, will You help him to see it?" "How does it feel?" "How true does this sound to that little boy . . . ?" "What would it mean if . . . ?" "Let yourself just drift back to a time when you first felt that . . . " "Jesus, will You show him when . . . ?"[6]

"Well . . . I feel like my life is on sort of a downward spiral, and there is nothing I can do about it. Like I am on a slide and at the end something terrible or violent will happen. It gives me nightmares. I write about it in my journal and try to draw it. It's like the things I want to do with my life will never happen. It really depresses me. It's hopeless, inevitable, failure, just . . . " His voice trailed off.

Almost suddenly, as if some sunlight pierced through the clouds, the foggy veil of deceit began to lift, and the chessboard battle over Ben's life was exposed. Van Gogh met a tragic, driven, artsy end. Insanity and confusion reigned in his last days, and eventual suicide. But the side of van Gogh few know was his early strong and rugged love for the oppressed, and his desire to be an evangelist. But darkness pulled him under, and the rest of his life was a slow descent into that evil even while his artistic ability flourished.

In an instant God had drawn the battle lines and the victory plan and conveyed it all in a simple fleeting picture.

And, when gently mentioned, even in hopeful ignorance, that picture coming from a stranger challenged both Ben's feelings that God was distantly unconcerned and his own lack of any hope for change. What a setup. How powerful is our God, our Wonderful Counselor, our Partner!

Ben sat up and looked me in the eye.

"What's going on?" he asked.

"I'm not sure. Let's see, okay?"

"Sure . . . why not?"

Ben's true destiny, set before the world's foundation, was just the opposite of the evil intention of his and God's enemy. A year or two earlier Ben had hitchhiked across a dangerous foreign frontier to serve displaced refugees, braving mountain roads and bandits. He had always gone after the ragged poor where only the rugged child of God could thrive. He was drawn to it, made for it. Oppression of the poor or helpless incensed him.

Fueled by anger and rebellion against a perceived distant father, a doorway of deception opened. Masquerading as unalterable truth, the lies anchored in pain propped up a whole false card house, all carefully placed, sounding true but full of treachery: God was weak, it seemed, or worse, uninterested, and the inner world of his soul was a dark and hopeless place—maybe better to leave it now.

We asked Jesus what He thought about that and He spoke to Ben: "You're My mountain climber. I trust you in tough places. We're roped together so you won't fall."

"Is that just me thinking those words?" Ben asked.

"Do *you* think it was just you?"

"No. That is the *last* thing I would have thought!"

"Me either. Do they sound true to you?"

"Oh, yes!"

Then he saw it. A "violent end" like that of van Gogh's was *not* inevitable! Fear of personal and unavoidable catastrophe was *not* in control. He *did* have a future and a hope . . . even a wonderful destiny. *That* was what was inevitable. We shared a Scripture or two. He saw it clearly and it brought out the fight in him.

Forgiveness for a distant and unconcerned father was given freely. The lie was renounced. Papa God is not at all like that. The power of the enemy of Providence was broken. The command to leave was given. Ben himself spoke it with a strong voice.

We spoke truth along with destiny blessing. Dave began to speak to him about his life, and you could see Ben's spirit swelling like a sponge, soaking in warm, wonderful truth. He saw it. He is a rugged servant warrior, the other side of van Gogh. Lots of tears, a few big yawns, a little shake and . . . firstfruits of freedom. He felt a dark weight leave him. "You will know the truth, and the truth will set you free."

The foolishness of God is wiser than the wisdom of men.[7] God's unusual ways and gentle, nondirective words were allowed to flow through knuckleheaded kids who knew they had little to give but lots to offer if they would risk foolishness.

I told him, "Ben, you still have the opportunity to think that old way, but no longer the obligation; your choice."

Ben walked away that day believing something different. How it worked out in daily life? I frankly don't fully know. Good thing Ben was now connected with God, and saw Him in a new light. He knew who he was and it resonated deep within him.

Hope was back.

Ben needed to "lay hold of that for which he was laid hold of" for sure. Nothing of that magnitude is won without a dark demonic probing at a later time. Rarely is a pondering mind totally changed instantly . . . but he now knew he could get a grip, and that there was a powerful ally on his side. His small group of friends could now come around him with the purpose of being a support to him. As his mind grew more comfortable with the changed view of reality, slow or fast, he himself would change on the outside.

Ben is a picture of what we see all the time—one young man, two plans for his life—one a dark fate, one a bright destiny. There is much more here than meets the eye.

The Blueprint of a Man

God indicates to us that He has designed each person with a specially purposed life, with numbered days, with specific equipping or gifting and with unique works prepared for him or her to co-accomplish with God.[8]

Papa God nudges you, sometimes in advance, sometimes right at that instant and says, "Hey, I'm about to do something fun...want to come?" And when you say "yes," almost always at a bit of risk to your comfort zone, you experience His presence and friendship. Doing it *together* is His highest pleasure.

You do not have to try out or interview for these nudge moments. You were made for them.

You are it.

There is much more at stake beneath the surface of this plan and way of God than simply finding your "call." You are part of an unseen plan of God, one of intergalactic conquest! If you look back carefully you will begin to connect the dots and see His nudges are not random. It is a careful plan and blueprint to grow you into, well, *yourself.* Paul calls it "from glory to glory."[9]

In Paul's letter to the Ephesians, he says that you carry something of the essence of God that is unique to you. It is called your *metron* in the Greek, your "measure of God."[10] One person seemingly exudes His gentleness, another His laughter and humor, another His mercy, and so on. Ben exhibited His rugged "go anywhere, pay any price" love. When left to himself, he naturally gravitated toward assignments and activities that took him there. It gave him a sense of fullness and of adventure.

When each of us operates within our *metron*, the Bible says that Jesus' body will "measure" up to the fullness of Christ. Millions of fully functional mini-Jesus men and women, delivered on earth with some assembly required to be fully Jesus. That is God's plan for conquest.

And our enemy detests the whole idea.

The Evil Plan

The devil hates God. Let's face it.

Negotiations will not solve it. It is a never-ending, diabolical, seething, jealous rage. There is no treaty or truce.

You and your *metron* (God in you) represent a risk to Satan's hold on part of planet Earth—your part. The assault of Satan's demons is *not* random. It is not just some chance "wheel of misfortune." On the contrary, the aggressive and singular objective of hell's forces is to find an approach that will somehow neutralize (at least) and totally pervert and destroy (at most) the place of intended glory in a man or woman. He attempts to pervert and destroy the very aspect of each person that is planned to display the grace and glory of God to the rest of the world: the *metron* of Jesus in you—your destiny and calling.

And if he can add torment, harassment, injustice, pain and wounding—all the better. And that is our fourth foundation overall, and the second foundation about the evil one.

FOUNDATION #4—

Issues are not random.

Once you attune to it, it is everywhere apparent. Look around. Start close to home. It is generational, it is pervasive and it is deadly effective.

1. God is good. Satan is bad.
2. Your freedom is God's will.
3. We have hidden enemies.
4. Issues are not random.
5. There is always a reason.
6. Prisoners and captives.
7. Partners with God.
8. A culture of honor.
9. Apply God's solutions.
10. An event and a process.

A Few Examples

Fred—the Daring Leader

Fred was designed by God to have a strong practical capability and daring leadership. He was meant to be the one everyone turned to when they needed practical know-how. But Fred's father was so belittling that Fred deeply believed that he was worthless and inept. And as he believed in his heart, so it flowed out into the world. He was unsure, timid and failing. Evil's scheme was to beat Fred into cowering submission when young, thus assuring his incapacitation as a man. His tactic was to bring authorities into his life that were harsh and judging. Mistakes were painful experiences. Fred believed that in the world in which he lived, to try and fail resulted in great pain . . . and he seemed to fail at everything. So why try?

But God had other plans.

When Fred truly saw what had happened, and when God spoke to him about his strengths, Fred actually got angry and we began to see a strong tenacity rise up in him. Today he is well on his way to becoming what he is called to be: capable, trusted, dependable, loving. He is the go-to guy for many in our congregation.

Monica—the Listener to God

Monica was strongly "prophetic." In the New Age she would be an Indigo Child—seeing deeply, restless about society, hearing with two sets of ears and double-sighted. Even as a young girl she would see and say things that seemed almost otherworldly . . . if you believed in that sort of thing.

Which Monica's parents certainly did not.

She told her parents she saw angels. Her parents laughed uncomfortably at her "fantasy." When she persisted, they subtly shut her up and quietly shut her down. They then practiced benign neglect in Monica's spiritual upbringing.

And she slowly starved. When a teenager, her church let her know that she was out of bounds, and somehow "wrong," as a woman trying to speak up.

Monica was badly wounded, and she eventually developed a condescending attitude toward authority, a biting way and an angry path. She went in circles. Her insights allowed her to see motives and hearts. Yet her pain and anger caused her to judge everyone around her, and so she was inevitably judged in return. She was the master at cynically pointing out sin and inconsistency, but she failed at seeing God's good plan for the revelatory insight she was given and at cooperating with a gentle Papa to bring about healing and change. She had no grid in which to put tender and enthusiastic encouragement. If Satan cannot directly stop the gifting and calling, he will pervert it.

God did an end run around Monica's well-developed defenses built carefully to protect the sensitive little girl within. The Sozo team began to weep uncontrollably over Monica, apologizing for not keeping their "Sozo face." She melted and cried with them, sobbing over the hurting and confused little girl she knew still cowered inside. Her defenses gave up their hard job.

God began to nurture and father her, to call out her best, to teach her that someone with insight like hers can work with God to bring about the *intention,* not simply the *information*; that *relation* is as important as *revelation.* She confessed and repented. She gave up the lie that she was mistrusted and different, and that she needed to act out of wounding. Papa spoke wonderfully to her as we watched in awe. She forgave her parents and pastors. Monica grew and softened rapidly.

Bill—Gentle and Strong

Bill was a lover.

He was gentle, sensitive and musical. His father was not. That was a big problem for both of them. Sports were not on Bill's agenda. Sunday afternoons were a hellish struggle between the Final Four and the string quartet. Misunderstood and rejected, Bill ended up crushed, abandoned and broken. He turned to pornography for relief and other sexual behavior at odds with God's best. He listened to dark music, composed morbidly sad songs and wrote murky poetry. He contemplated suicide. The enemy hates the artistic ones most of all, for they most fully express Lucifer's old job: worship.[11]

God spoke to Bill in a tender way: *You are My son. I love to cuddle with you and to make up "silly story songs" with you.* It was wording his father had used when he was very young and they lay together in bed after being tucked in. How God dissolved his heart then. "He knows . . . He knows." His eyes filled with tears of wonder. "God really knows and understands me, doesn't He?"

Bill knew then he was okay; that he was strong, and that macho was not the way he expressed his strength; that meekness was strength under control, and that Jesus was proud of him. We watched as Bill and God cried together, sobbing and shaking. That night Papa pulled the cork on the bottled-up poison of hatred, and much of the pain drained out. Forgiveness and removing of judgment about Dad brought a flood of tears and longing. And we held him for a long time, Papa soothing his heart while we prayed. Confession of sin brought more tears of shame, and Papa let him know He understood and did not condemn him . . . not even a little. He gave it to Jesus in exchange for purity. It is not about sin . . . it never is in the end.

Bill is now walking out the new freedom he has found, and is blossoming in art and music, writing a children's musical . . . filled with silly story songs.

Application in Your World

Every person has his or her own unique story . . . Ben, Fred, Monica, Bill . . . you. We often come to see the hidden pattern of evil and the intent of good. It is not random, and it is normally hidden. We can expose the hidden plan of the evil one, nullify the bad and call forth the good, helping to instill vision and focus and put the fight back into the warrior.

Perhaps even now you can see some of the pattern of resistance and the evil structures that have been arrayed against you. You have a hidden enemy. But do not be dismayed—as you will discover shortly, you have a not-so-hidden ally.

My child, listen to me . . . Papa loves you. Think about that one. Reread chapter 2. Climb up on His lap, lean your head against His chest, hear His heartbeat, sigh and rest. You have an exciting walk with Him. And it is never too late to take His hand and say, "Yes, You bet I want to come!"

4

Two Foundations about Us

All human beings should try to learn before they die what they are running from, and to, and why.

James Thurber

The highest possible stage in moral culture is when we recognize that we ought to control our thoughts.

Charles Darwin

We see the world not as it is but as we are.

Stephen Covey

Ignorance is voluntary misfortune.

Nicholas Ling

Cause and Effect in the Real World

Sir Isaac Newton was right.

For every action there is an equal and opposite reaction. In the lives of men there are some obvious natural, logical and psychological causes and effects. But there is also another dynamic, one that bursts into the world of men, that is fueled by that other world, where God and devils dwell. Here is one of my favorites.

So, it is the third year of famine in Israel. People are suffering.

David asks God what is going on. Maybe it took that long to decide it was not *just* a bad year or two . . . or three. When David asks God, He answers and says a strange thing. He says the famine is caused by the previous king's recent poor treatment of the Gibeonites. Saul broke an ill-advised covenant made with a dishonest tribe by Joshua four hundred years earlier.[1]

Four hundred years!

That is twice as old as the United States.

Gracious, who is supposed to know *that*!

The fact that Joshua never asked God about making the covenant in the first place does not seem to enter at all into the cause-effect dynamic. The fact that David and the people of Israel did not remember the covenant or notice Saul's mistreatment were also not a factor in easing the suffering— God remembered, and so did Satan. A covenant had been made, a vow spoken. Until it was honored the famine would continue.

Here's another one.

Simon (a.k.a. Peter) is warned that Satan has demanded to sift him like wheat. Jesus' response is to pray for him that he does not give up.[2] Why didn't Jesus just protect Simon? This whole dynamic seems strange until you begin to think about Simon's previous behavior and make some inferences. The demanded sifting might just be because of the door of dark invitation he opened through his arrogant pride in judging everyone else's cowardice and disputing for the prime spot in the Kingdom.[3] Simon finally repents after a servant girl calls his blustering bluff, and he is restored by Jesus to his destiny call and the premier position he is now qualified to handle after all. In the way you judge you will be judged.[4] Judas Iscariot faced similar testing by Satan with a darker result. [5]

Jesus tells the crippled man who had been sitting at the pool of Bethesda for 38 years to sin no more "so that nothing worse happens to you."[6] What happened 38 years earlier?

In the world of men there is a tendency (some say a law) toward sowing and reaping, cause and effect. It is portrayed throughout Scripture. You see it as the result of both an individual decision and of group choices, of self-inflicted torment and as that perpetrated by another. A reaction is caused by an action. An *ongoing* reaction remains because the action has not been dealt with and still churns out its poison. It is part and parcel of this world—you will have tribulation. And it all started somewhere. That is the first foundation about us.

FOUNDATION #5—

There is always a reason.

The pain, failure, hindrance, sin or demonic torment in a person's life had a source, a beginning point, an origin. It may not have been the person's doing at all, but that of someone against them. But there *was* a cause to bring about the effect, an action that brought the painful or harmful reaction.

Paul explains it succinctly:

1. God is good. Satan is bad.
2. Your freedom is God's will.
3. We have hidden enemies.
4. Issues are not random.
5. **There is always a reason.**
6. Prisoners and captives.
7. Partners with God.
8. A culture of honor.
9. Apply God's solutions.
10. An event and a process.

Do not be deceived, God is not mocked; for whatever a man sows, this he will also reap. For the one who sows to his own flesh will from the flesh reap corruption, but the one who sows to the Spirit will from the Spirit reap eternal life.

Galatians 6:7–8

This propensity is somehow a part of the fabric of God's created universe. It is not, as some would have it, a totally impersonal balancing of the forces of yin and yang of the I Ching, or a mechanistic reexperiencing of good and bad karma repaid in a later life. It is not just the "Law of Attraction" as portrayed in *The Secret*.

But *all* truth is God's truth and this tendency is real nonetheless. Sin has consequences.[7] Righteousness has rewards.[8] Faith moves mountains. There are *both* current-world *and* next-world results of our choices and beliefs for good and for bad.[9]

God's original plan for men and women was that everyone would reap the blessed fruit of past generations and pass along a multiplied blessing to our children. Age to age, generation to generation, multiplied, ever-increasing, never-ending blessing.

Then we gave it away in Eden.

In the world we will have tribulation, pressure, issues, pains, hurts and failures. Each of us is subject to fallout from these things. We are each culpable and each victimized, each swept up to a greater or lesser extent by the forces at play around and within us. We are each acting out the natural/supernatural consequences of the "there is always a reason" principle.

Time, by itself, never heals wounds, never erases sin, never eliminates the cause and never casts out the demonic. It only makes us forget what it is that put us in prison in the first place, and what is killing us. We become inured to the low level of existence, used to the pain. We go "three years with famine" in our own land unaware of the cause-effect dynamic playing itself out. It is bottled in ignorance,

68

lies and forgetfulness—but it stays fresh until exposed to the light.

Cause and Effect Examples

Here are some examples of cause and effect that are commonly experienced. Every one of the examples is real; only the names have been changed.

- Fred cannot relate to authority due to a brutal father.
- Mary is afraid to ride in a car due to an accident as a young girl.
- Betty felt she could not measure up to her mother's expectations and quit trying—becoming a rebel.
- June's daughter will not talk to her due to June's unforgiveness of her.
- Dave feels a sense of resistance in relationships and hindrance in his career shown to be due to his unforgiveness toward his father.
- Ralph hopes his dad suffers like he suffered—judging him but not knowing his dad was abused as a child. But he feels others judge him and are avoiding him.
- Ken steals from his company and experiences economic malaise in his life.
- Barry is a habitual liar and never seems to find a place to land in life.
- George cannot relate sexually to his wife due to the pornography he indulges in.
- Guilt haunts Betty due to a sexual fling she had while on a trip. It has caused her marriage to fail.
- Tim is afraid of failure and constantly reads more and more to try to insure he knows more than those around him.

- Bob's retirement account is his safety net, and he is constantly anxious about the market.

- Megan is controlled by her mother's expectations, and this illicit soul tie has ruined her marriage.

- Mike is afraid all the time, and it all stemmed from his neighbor, who sexually molested him and threatened to kill his parents if he said anything.

- Kelly vowed she would never be like her mother and feels a sense of loss and detachment in life.

- Henry made an inner agreement to accept the offer of protection from a friendly guide (really a demon) when he was four and terrorized at night. Now he feels controlled and fearful.

- Hank brought home some dark artifacts and masks from Africa and now experiences a strange dark feeling, headaches and stomach pains.

- Kendra frequented a fortune-teller and now experiences whispering voices and night terrors.

- Len's dad said he would never amount to anything, and Len has been affected by that ever since.

- Cary constantly says he cannot control himself, and his negative self-speak plays itself out in his life.

- Ken joined an organization that required him to repeat curses concerning his family and his life. Now those vows are being played out in his children.

- Don's ancestors were violent racists, and he and his kin have experienced judgment, violence and failure.

- Debbie's mother was not married when she got pregnant and was terribly anxious throughout the pregnancy. Debbie has trouble with her nerves and seems "high strung" and unable to cope with life.

- Terry's parents did not want a fourth child. He came into the world feeling unguided.

Prisoners and Captives

In looking at the examples above you may have noticed something, and that something is the second foundation about us. You might have reacted to some of the examples saying, "Oh, that poor person," and to others, "Well, they seemed to get what they deserved." Setting aside for a moment the fact that we cannot unerringly make such omniscient judgments, it does seem true that there are basically two kinds of issues—those we bring on ourselves and those that others perpetrate on us.

Jesus quotes this about Himself:[10]

> The Spirit of the Lord GOD is upon me, because the LORD has anointed me to bring good news to the afflicted; He has sent me to bind up the brokenhearted, to proclaim liberty to captives and freedom to prisoners.
>
> Isaiah 61:1

Liberty to captives, freedom to prisoners. This distinction is important to freedom.

- *Captives* have been captured in war through no fault of their own. They are held in bondage due to wounding and the resultant false or unfruitful beliefs. Their surface behavior can be confusing, sinful or full of issues that must be dealt with. But their sin is a *reaction* to wounding.
- *Prisoners* are held in prison because they have done something to deserve it. They are held until they are granted pardon. Most prisoners are in a self-made prison of sin, self-binding actions (such as vows or covenants) or unforgiveness.[11] They hold the key to freedom, and can reverse the results of their actions.

This is the second foundation about us.

FOUNDATION #6—

Prisoners and captives.

Becoming a Prisoner or a Captive   *Wrong!*

1. God is good. Satan is bad.
2. Your freedom is God's will.
3. We have hidden enemies.
4. Issues are not random.
5. There is always a reason.
6. **Prisoners and captives.**
7. Partners with God.
8. A culture of honor.
9. Apply God's solutions.
10. An event and a process.

At our core we were created to need God's love and presence. As in the picture in figure 2, God's plan is to have protective boundaries around the heart of every child—just like our physical skin is to our body. Parents, grandparents and others are intended to work with God to protect us when we are young. It is God's intent that they leave us a godly legacy and help bring us into His presence and our destiny in Him. We were meant to be safe and blessed.

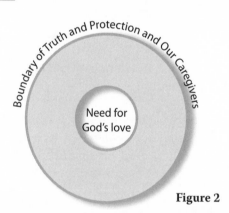

Boundary of Truth and Protection and Our Caregivers

Need for God's love

Figure 2

As we age we take on more and more personal responsibility under God and develop our own skin of godly protection through believing truth, in proper relationship with friends and family and under proper authority. God meets that inner need through His wonderful fatherly presence and that of Jesus and the Holy Spirit.[12]

But we live in a fallen world. At specific points in time, sin or trauma attempt to break those boundaries. Temptation and resulting sin *invite* (Prisoner—out-swinging door); trauma and wounding *invade* (Captive—in-swinging door). Generational issues or ungodly foundational lies can be passed on to us. Wounding of our spirits can occur even in the womb. (See figure 3.) *Agree*

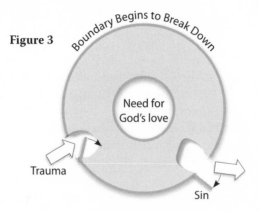

Figure 3

When we are very young our own sin is not the issue as much as invasion—the sin of others against us. We are captives who are hurt and confused when bad things happen to us. It feels wrong to our childlike spirits, and we seek for resolution and relief. In so doing we often create an inner reality, or belief paradigm, out of the few things we already know and what we are now presented with. Our minds are amazingly adept at creating a plausible explanation for the "reality" we perceive around us, and in finding ways to cope with that world. The mind finds resolution for the heart's confusion.

If our God-appointed protections are doing their job, it is nipped in the bud by an alert parent. When we are young, our parents work with God to build foundations of truth within us, and we can, even early on, choose truth over lies. If the demonic is present, it will offer devious lies and false comforts to explain and resolve what is happening. As a young child we don't know much, so even seemingly minor events can have a big impact on us. The dynamic shown in figure 4 begins to take place.

Figure 4

Without that protection dynamic, events are explained by demonically inspired lies. Our consideration of these lies causes us to react in fearful, self-protective or sinful ways. Repeated and strengthened, these form beliefs within us. The strengthening or intertwining of multiple false beliefs, perhaps abetted by demons, creates a darkly defensible stronghold within us.

Most of the time, as young children, the fact that we are presented with a choice, good or bad, dark or light, is very subtle and hidden. In many situations a child, in reality, has little obvious choice because the "truth and love" alternative may be scarcely present or perceived. The demonic offers comfort, protection or the fulfillment of some other felt need. Or it terrorizes and intimidates into submission. It is not fair, but it happens.

When we are very young we create core beliefs about ourselves, others, our environment and God. Core lies form, too. These lies are held at the deepest emotional and subconscious level—in the heart. They then propel reactions, actions and decisions.[13] Core lies in our lives often center around two key areas: victimization and rejection.[14] Almost everybody has dealt with some form of these two:[15]

Victimization

Powerlessness—"I am a helpless victim of others and can't protect myself."

Fear—"The world and people in it are not safe for me."

Personal Tainting—"I am scarred and ruined forever by what has happened."

Hopelessness—"It is terrible and will never get better."

Confusion—"I cannot find peace and understanding in my world."

Rejection

Shame—"I am sinful and dirty and deserve punishment."

Rejection—"The ones I need reject me because I am not worth loving."

Identity Invalidation—"Who I am is not right nor worth paying attention to."

Disaffirmation—"I am worthless, unattractive and stupid and deserve to be ignored."

Abandonment—"Those I love and need will abandon me."

As we mature we become responsible for decisions we make and sin becomes possible. We may be predisposed to making sinful choices due to the foundations that have been laid. If we choose truth, by ourselves or with help, then healing results, the doors are shut and we move on—strengthened and maturing in our ability to respond appropriately to negative experiences. The previous lies are eventually overcome by truth.

Left to themselves, however, believed lies and wounded reactions begin to dominate and constrain parts of us—as shown in figure 5. Aided and abetted by demons, they create a false barrier against pain—one of self-protection, deception and limitation. Within that wall, darkness begins to grow.

As *prisoners*, we continue to seek the pleasure of a sinful habit or addiction, believing that the sin gives us what we need—thus becoming more and more controlled and warped to serve it. We move into ever-deeper bondage transitioning from suggestion or situation, to impression, to oppression, to obsession. Along the way we lose more and more

Figure 5

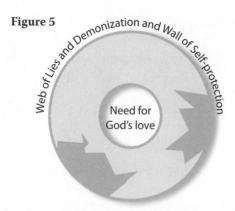

freedom, spiritual lucidity and rationality. The demonic goal is destruction.

As *captives* we can respond to wounding aggressively (anger, rage, bitterness, outbursts and even murder) or passively (self-pity, withdrawal, self-hatred and even suicide). Sometimes our responses are only marginally controllable. Some behaviors are designed to protect the person from his pain or provide a solution to it: addictions, ritualized actions, anorexia, homosexuality, etc. They are pain-management coping mechanisms. Other behaviors are the direct result or consequence of the pain and sin: phobias, panic reactions, etc.

A person then either tries to arrange their life in reaction to, or avoidance of, these painful areas—thus becoming more and more bound and isolated, and less and less in control. Defense mechanisms, ways of acting and relating, can form and begin to limit our freedom. In some cases mild dissociation is the protection of choice. In more severe cases dissociation can mean survival, leading to more complex issues beyond the scope of first responder training.

This web of deception, sin and wounding, created over time in an unsuspecting life, is called a "stronghold." It feels hopeless and unchangeable. That place, or those places, may be inhabited by the demonic—a base of operations. The person may be normal in most other ways, but when this

Sarah "inordinate"

area is touched or encountered, we see unusually strong and inappropriate reactions. It is an echo of what has happened in the past. We have walked into a minefield of old pain and anger. Whether it is demonic presence or simply handiwork, the area seems to have a life and energy of its own.

Inside, the person still has a need for God's love and presence.

They may come into experiences of love and salvation and find respite for periods of time. They may marry and have children and lead normal lives.

The ability to cope with the inner turmoil often starts to break down later in life. We may begin to grow aware of constraints in our lives, quirks and flaws in our personalities and behavior, things we take for granted but in actuality do not square with the Bible or the beliefs of well-adjusted people around us. Neither God nor the demonic will leave us static, but with opposite intent. Things begin to happen. Perhaps a crisis comes about and we grow desperate. Maybe a friend confronts us or a spouse wants to go to counseling. An understanding emerges that "something is really wrong inside me."

The person begins to look for help and a good friend to talk to as the first line of defense, the first responder.

Maybe it is you.

Uses "constraints" rather than "barriers"

Application in Your World

To close this chapter, let me reiterate these two foundational principles boldly and without equivocation. *Everything* that you have done or has been done against you that has, as intrinsic to its nature, stealing, killing and destroying is not from God and is fair game to be gotten rid of.

It had a source and origin apart from God's foundational plan for you. It is not God's intent for a harmful issue to dominate your life—either as a prisoner or as a captive. He knows the reason or cause. He is willing to help you find it and to begin experiencing freedom in that area. If the discussion above seems daunting, remember this: Your role is *not* to try to unravel and sort out all the tangles of someone's life. That is God's job. Your role is simply to partner with God in the one thing He brings to light.

It is time to turn the corner and talk about God's solution to all this mess. So saddle up and let's learn how to become partners with God.

5

Two Foundations about Being a First Responder

For we are God's fellow workers; you are God's field, God's building.

1 Corinthians 3:9

Pray as if everything depended upon God, and work as if everything depended upon man.

Francis Cardinal Spellman

There are three stages in the work of God: impossible, difficult, done.

James Hudson Taylor

I Will Go with You

I love the part in *The Lion King* movie when the hyenas are about to devour the two cubs that had strayed into their territory. In desperation the lion cub Simba rears back to roar and this powerful hair-raising bellow booms forth. Only it is not Simba but Mufasa the lion king who, standing behind Simba, does it all. I feel like that many times when ministering to someone—as does anyone who knows that in the end, it is God who does the heavy lifting. It seems to be God's way if we will let Him.

God calls Moses to go to Egypt, and this very funny dialog ensues:[1]

> God: "*I* am concerned about My people in Egypt, so I am sending *you*, Moses."
>
> Moses: "Who am I?"
>
> God: "I'll go with you."
>
> Moses: "Then who are You?"
>
> God: "I AM."
>
> Moses: "Oh, boy."

If you look at the life of any God-chosen biblical character, you will see a common thread: Abraham (Genesis 15:1), Jacob (Genesis 31:3), Moses (Exodus 3:12), Joshua (Joshua 1:5), Nehemiah (Nehemiah 2:8), Isaiah (Isaiah 41:10), David (Psalm 23:4), Solomon (1 Chronicles 28:20), the disciples (Mark 16:20), early Christians (Acts 11:21) and . . . us forever (Matthew 28:20). God's final answer to any question about His calling of every person into any kind of ministry situation is, "I'll go with you."

1. God is good. Satan is bad.
2. Your freedom is God's will.
3. We have hidden enemies.
4. Issues are not random.
5. There is always a reason.
6. Prisoners and captives.
7. **Partners with God.**
8. A culture of honor.
9. Apply God's solutions.
10. An event and a process.

Paul says we are "co-workers" with God, who causes the growth.[2] That is us. And that is the first important foundation about how we minister.

FOUNDATION #7—

Partners with God.

Being in intimate partnership with the infinite, omniscient, omnipresent creator of the universe can be stretching!

80

God is not human. He says to us, "You and I are incompatible . . . and I don't change."[3] His ways are way, way above ours, and He enjoys making foolish the wisdom of the world.[4] That does not mean we do not study, work, pray and think hard. But it *does* mean that, in the end, our weight comes down on trusting God, not training, experience or technique—and on agreeing to be stretched.

That is a narrow road to walk. It is never either/or. The ditch on one side is reliance on training and technique. "God gave us our brains and the Word and we operate out of that." Operating that way leads to results that are often limited to my skill and knowledge. That is best left for trained counselors who *have* skill and knowledge. Why do I need God? People encounter me and my good suggestions. But what they hunger for is an encounter with God.

In the other ditch is some sort of "woo-woo" hyper-spirituality bordering on Christian voodoo and, frankly, lots of nonsense. We make crazy, unverifiable, unbiblical pronouncements couched in prophetic jargon, say a few prayers and send someone off hopeful but often destined to disappointment.

When we find the sweet spot in the middle as co-laborers, God is willing to enter into a partnership with us even when we are not perfectly suited to Him and His ways. He will find ways to work through almost any good-hearted individual with true compassion for the person in need and willing to listen and obey. Among our teams and individuals who experience this kind of ministry, it is a given that we are all just taking notes on the Holy Spirit. We refer almost all questions to Jesus.

Jesus walked this way.

He said only what He currently heard the Father saying, did what He currently saw the Father doing. This pleased the Father.[5] That is very different from reliance on a carefully rehearsed five-step process—though the five-step process given in this book may be the framework in which you operate. Thus, my primary preparation is to spend time knowing God and His voice. Secondarily I read, study, learn, watch, ask, cogitate and meditate. If it was good enough for the Son of God . . .

So how do we do that?

The Voice of God and Ministry: Voices and Screens

Some think it is presumption to expect God to speak to you in a ministry setting. We think it is presumption not to.

In Sozo ministry we *anticipate* God will speak. We *expect* we will listen.

This can feel intimidating to us . . . all of us. It is actually not hard, but is natural and intuitive to most people, even nonbelievers. If you are now a believer in Jesus, then this is true: When you were a rebellious and confused sinner, you heard God clearly enough to decide to turn to Him; how much more now that you are His dear child do you hear His voice? He even unequivocally declares that fact.[6]

Many have dismissed the whole idea of this inner-spiritual world as "spiritual babble" or shied away from it as too dangerous and subjective. Others have plunged into it in total naïveté, not realizing the potential dangers in unbounded and unguided openness. There is a safe way to navigate our inner sanctum, and finding the balance between the two mind-sets is crucial to ministering healing and freedom. Almost always the key to understanding our constraining and painful issues and the most direct route to freedom is found within that world.

As Jesus stated clearly, we can trust God to protect us and guide us as we faithfully and honestly call on Him:

> "So I say to you, ask, and it will be given to you; seek, and you will find; knock, and it will be opened to you. For everyone who asks, receives; and he who seeks, finds; and to him who

knocks, it will be opened. Now suppose one of you fathers is asked by his son for a fish; he will not give him a snake instead of a fish, will he? Or if he is asked for an egg, he will not give him a scorpion, will he? If you then, being evil, know how to give good gifts to your children, how much more will your heavenly Father give the Holy Spirit to those who ask Him?"

Luke 11:9–13

The fact is, we all rely on hearing God. Every pastor, no matter how dispensational or conservative, wants to be breathed into, or "inspired." Every Christian, no matter how immature, wants God to "help" them in their endeavors. So the only real disagreement in this discussion comes when we seek to understand just how specific and pointed that communication can be. I once argued with a Ph.D. seminary graduate about this for five hours. His position was that God gave us minds and we should use them to analyze the Word and then teach it. He then stated he needed to go pray for *in*sight and *in*spiration for his upcoming sermon. We both stopped and smiled. "God gotcha," I said.

I like to explain it to our newer Sozo ministers in terms of three voices and three screens.

Jesus, referring to the Holy Spirit, said that out of our inner being will flow rivers of living water.[7] Continuous, natural, not forced. We can learn to honor and place weight on the flow of God and discern between:[8]

- Our own minds—derived from stored information, more analytical and soulish;
- Demonic suggestion—harsh, manipulative, dark and slimy; and
- God's voice along with that of our spirits—alive, fresh, weighty, unexpected, full of energy, revelatory and insightful.

Those voices come to our attention through one of three internal "flat screen televisions" of input that come into our souls (mind, will and emotions) and to which we can choose to pay attention.[9] (See figure 6.) They are the screens of:

- *Senses and Drives*—This screen monitors body function and external sensory input. Its voice says, "I'm hungry," or, "Look at that red balloon!"
- *Memory and Analysis*—This screen monitors output from our minds and draws on our memories. We can be asked to recall a favorite birthday present and immediately a picture of the gift appears on that screen. It is also the screen on which the results of internal analysis are played out. We need to balance our checkbook, and the ability to do math (along with some painful memories of algebra!) is displayed on that screen.
- *Imagination and Impression*—This screen creates images of things never previously experienced but suggested by others or requested by the soul. Someone could say, "Imagine yourself on the moon," and you could instantly be there. Just as quickly you could transport yourself to the top of Mount Everest in your mind's eye. It is also the channel of much inspiration and the flow of intuitive creativity. It monitors input bubbling up from our spirits in the form of impressions, pictures, words, thoughts, feelings, etc.

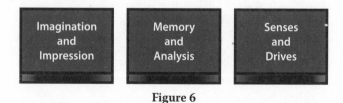

Figure 6

God can speak on any one of those screens, and, in fact, they all flow together to some extent. This differentiation is just for understanding. For example, He uses external things, touching them with significance and bringing them to our notice on the screen of senses and drives—people, books, objects, nature, "coincidences," memories, bodily sensations, etc.

He brings to mind (the screen of memory and analysis) a specific memory that, stored for years, suddenly has "sauce" on it. Each person is different and uniquely relates to God in infinite variation. But in every case, for something to carry weight or significance, it still must have His light shined on it and catch our attention.

In many people God chooses and uses the screen of imagination and impression because it can often be the most flexible and amenable for His input. He speaks to us in a form superior to actual written or oral speech. He, from our spirits, causes a "flow" to bubble up from within us.

God's answers are wiser than our questions.

We rarely get only what we expect. Often God's answers bring about a transformation of heart, not a transfer of information. The rich young ruler asks Jesus a theological question, and He gives a heart-targeted reply addressing the man's real issue of insecurity and riches-based idolatry.[10] The woman at the well wants to know where is the best place to worship, and Jesus tells her it's within her spirit—and then addresses her real heart need.[11]

Sometimes His answers point to issues of destiny, identity, belief or relations. Sometimes the answers are so deep and yet so simple that they compel the person to greater faith, making them desperate for freedom, and stir up desire for intimacy with the One who communicated His love in such a telling way. Sometimes God's communications are symbolic, leading to deeper revelation, amazing self-insight and tears or even humor. Papa or Jesus often says things with a knowing, kind and even wry smile. We have seen God cover shame and guilt with gentle warm humor.

Good! Questions

Quest. to ask

But we can miss it.

We can misinterpret His voice. That's okay. That is where humility and compassion come in handy. That is why we, as ministers, offer only pictures or thoughts that come on to *our* screens as suggestions ("Does van Gogh mean anything to you?") and only when we sense permission to do so.

In our ministry settings, we often ask an individual to close their eyes, to be still and to report what they are "seeing, hearing or sensing." We ask God if He has input on specific questions and concerns, or ask if He would like to do, say, indicate or show something. We anticipate an answer but it is totally okay if we sense nothing.

Never use guided imagery

We *never* use guided imagery where we set the stage and demand Jesus appear on it. We never make Jesus or anyone *do* anything—we always ask. We often just stop and say something like, "God, we are not sure what to do here; would You help us?" It is a little disconcerting to the person being ministered to at first. Then they normally start to enjoy it, knowing we are in this together and they can relax.

We can, for example, lead in the following ways:

* "Jesus, is there anything You want to show John that he believed about that event that was a lie from the devil?"

* "Jesus, John is feeling like that same wounded little boy. Is there anything You would want to tell him right now?"

* "God, would You help John get a picture of the wall that he feels might separate him from Your love or from relationship with others?"

* "Jesus, we're stuck, what are we missing? Will You help us?"

* "Papa, John is having trouble forgiving his dad right now. Will You help us?"

* "John, you know your body is a temple of the Holy Spirit. Let's ask God if there is anything in that temple that

doesn't belong there and is sort of an idol . . . in the way of His love reaching you . . . okay? Can you see yourself that way?"

✗ "John, are you having trouble letting God's love into this part of you? Let's ask Jesus if He would show us why."

To those who are more exclusively dependent on scientific psychodynamics or more traditional counseling approaches, this may seem overly subjective or even childish. We really respect and need those highly trained and experienced ones. But this is not counseling—it is two or three people coming together to ask God for His wisdom and counsel—partners with God.

We have found God to be an ever-present help in time of need. Is that overly subjective? Well, only so far as the scientific method cannot ascertain what is happening. But to the person receiving the pictures, senses, impressions or words from God, it is more real than anything else—and it has the power to set free and heal.

It never contradicts the Word . . . ever. And it is often a verse.

Here are some good and probably bad examples of this approach.

Proper use of memory, imagination and visualization	Improper use of memory, imagination and visualization
Letting God indicate if there is a memory that will give insight or other assistance in repenting, forgiving, knowing truth and letting go of wounding.	Always assuming that healing is found in the past, in a forgotten or suppressed memory or wounding inflicted by another.
Realizing, through God's leading, that our sin was partially a response to wounding and pain.	Blaming another for the sin in our life, avoiding the need for our own forgiving and repenting.

Proper use of memory, imagination and visualization	Improper use of memory, imagination and visualization
Holding a memory with an "open hand," knowing we do not always remember accurately.	Forcing recall and interpretation of details, planting thoughts and ideas, suggesting motives of others.
Asking God to bring to our memory an event that helped shape or form a particular issue, lie, belief or problem.	Forcing an interpretation on a memory or making it take on more significance than it may actually have.
Asking God to help us see a memory through His eyes or to interpret it as an adult with more maturity.	Asking God, or otherwise trying, to change what actually happened in a memory to make it more or less tolerable.
Asking God if He would be willing to show us something in a memory or if He has anything He would like to tell us.	Planting suggestions about what God "might want to do" or say. Telling God what to say or do.
Asking God what, if anything, He would like to say, indicate, show or do.	Telling God to say, indicate, show or do anything.
Using imagination as a vehicle to focus thought and listening for and to God.	Using imagination as a vehicle to create false memories or experiences, or as a way to force "Jesus" to show up.
Remembering that confession of and repentance from sin are central to biblical restoration and sanctification.	Reducing the impact of forgiveness and confession to a sidelight of ministry.

Get the difference?

Knowing that we are partners with God is key. It humbles and encourages at the same time. Now we will move to the second foundation about ministry: creating a culture of honor.

A Culture of Honor

I love reading testimonies of our ministry sessions. I like the ones that talk of powerful transformation, new light and freedom. But the ones I think I love the most are the ones like these:

- "I witnessed the love and compassion of God through men who were willing to listen and pray with me." (M.D.)
- "I am more aware of and secure in Jesus' love for me. He is always with me in an intimate way. I have encouraged all my friends to do this." (P.F.)
- "I always knew God loved me. But now I know He likes me! What a difference that makes!" (F.D.)
- "My daughter is not the same woman. Ten years of abuse had devastated her life. The gentleness of the women was amazing. My little girl is back. Thank You, Jesus!" (L.L.)
- "I had joy throughout the day and peace inside after my session. Fantastic!" (S.J.)

That is the heart of our Papa. Paul says:

> So, as those who have been chosen of God, holy and beloved, put on a heart of compassion, kindness, humility, gentleness and patience; bearing with one another, and forgiving each other, whoever has a complaint against anyone; just as the Lord forgave you, so also should you.
>
> Colossians 3:12–13

When someone says they felt honored, that they experienced kindness, gentleness, real love and compassion—some for the first time—that floats my boat.

When someone is vulnerable in our presence, confessing sin, weakness and the most intimate details of their failings, our response must be one of gentle understanding and true compassion.[12] This ministry is meant to be safe. It is confidential. We do not "kiss and tell." It is loving. It takes its time. It is one-on-one, face-to-face. People need to tell their story, to have a voice.

This is the second foundation about our ministry culture.

FOUNDATION #8—

1. God is good. Satan is bad.
2. Your freedom is God's will.
3. We have hidden enemies.
4. Issues are not random.
5. There is always a reason.
6. Prisoners and captives.
7. Partners with God.
8. **A culture of honor.**
9. Apply God's solutions.
10. An event and a process.

A culture of honor.

Practically, we ask permission to touch, to minister, to lead in prayer. Sometimes in a ministry setting we make popcorn. We stop and laugh. We know that the problem is the problem; the person is not the problem—and they know it, too. They know that we, God and they are all on one side of the table, and the issues—sin, wounding and everything else—are on the other side. God is not mad at them; He is having a good day.

We are not dupes. Do not misunderstand. We can be very direct. There is no place for false compassion and sinful compromise.

Putting These Two Foundations Together

So, we honor two things above all: the ways and flow of God, and vulnerable, hurting people. There are two verses that seem to balance one another and to sum up our approach to both honoring God's flow and vulnerable people:

> Do not quench the Spirit; do not despise prophetic utterances. But examine everything carefully; hold fast to that which is good; abstain from every form of evil.
>
> 1 Thessalonians 5:19–22

Let no unwholesome word proceed from your mouth, but only such a word as is good for edification according to the need of the moment, so that it will give grace to those who hear. Do not grieve the Holy Spirit of God, by whom you were sealed for the day of redemption.

Ephesians 4:29–30

Do not quench and do not grieve.

There is sometimes much to despise in what people today call "prophecy." In reality "prophecy" is just listening for God's voice and trying honorably and faithfully to convey that. It is for the purpose of forthtelling, not foretelling. It is for consolation, exhortation and edification.[13] God has nice things to say, and He uses people to say them. God has wise questions to ask, and He uses people to ask them.

Often the best use of our prophetic gifting is to more effectively lead and facilitate the session. Very often the key to unlocking a root cause, indicating destiny, releasing someone from a demonic stronghold or putting an exclamation mark on a time together is an insight from God. That's the upside. It is hard to grieve and quench when we are humbly pursuing God and honoring people.

The downside is that it is easy to grieve and quench through self-will. Do not grieve the Holy Spirit by blurting out any old thing that crosses your mind, but say only that which is suited for building another person up. Do not quench the Holy Spirit by despising the idea that God might be speaking through people to you or through you to others. Test and consider things carefully. Hold fast to the good. Let the other go without criticism. Correction can come later. Following those two rules makes all the difference. Do not grieve, do not quench—on both the sending and receiving end.

Here are some good and bad examples:

91

Good	Not so good
I feel like I am seeing a picture from third grade. Does that ring a bell at all?	Something happened to you in third grade.
Can I ask you about your past and present sexual experience?	You have a demon of lust.
Can I share with you a picture the Lord gave me at the beginning of our session that I wrote down? I think it will encourage you.	Before we start, I want to tell you what your problems are.
Can I help you connect the dots about what, to me, God seems to be saying today about a part of who you are?	You are supposed to be a preacher.
Can you see that this action seems to be a root for some of your current issues?	That sin is where it all began.
Wow! It seems to me that God has been talking today about that relationship. What are you hearing Him say?	God says that you are to break that relationship off.
I get this picture of you like a balloon rising into the sky. Does that register with you? It might be that God is saying you are like that in some way. Here's what I see in you like that . . .	You are a balloon rising into the sky.
Let's ask Jesus what He has to say about that, okay?	That's sin—no way!

Get the difference?

I was recently with someone who was very broken by a lifetime of sexual sin.

And I witnessed something amazing.

Mickey thought God was disgusted with him. We had showed him in Scripture that this was not so, and we prayed for him. He renounced, forgave, removed judgment and even coughed and spit for a minute after we rebuked a dark "friend" or two. He had trouble believing that God would talk to him—even when he spoke what he was hearing and sensing and it seemed to be powerful and insightful. He had lots of regret.

At the end, Terry, a frontline first responder and buddy of mine, said (with some inner trembling), "Mickey, I think God wants to give you a parting gift. Listen for a second and see if He wants to say anything to you."

After a bit of coaxing just to speak out the silly thoughts he heard, he said, "Well, I hear the word *significance*." Terry smiled and held up his notepad. Written in large block letters was the *very* word—*significance*. And underneath it were written three things about Mickey and his intended significance. Mickey looked puzzled at first, then stunned, then his mouth dropped open. A tear ran down his cheek, then he buried his face in his hands and sobbed—the neglected little boy who lost his significance with his father just found it afresh. That miracle, small and hidden in a church back room, changed him, and it convinced him that God is both real and loving.

Let's end with a quick summary. Scripture is clear about who is in charge, in the driver's seat, Captain of the vessel. This ministry is God's doing. We are the flight attendants making the passengers feel comfortable and safe.

Honor God.

Honor people.

Listen carefully with one ear in both worlds.

Smile.

Be nice.

Use breath mints!

6

Two Foundations about Tools and Process

Be diligent to present yourself approved to God as a workman who does not need to be ashamed, accurately handling the word of truth.

2 Timothy 2:15

Have thy tools ready. God will find thee work.

Charles Kingsley

One only needs two tools in life: WD-40 to make things go, and duct tape to make them stop.

G. Weilacher

There is nothing so powerful as truth—and often nothing so strange.

Daniel Webster

Tools

There are lots of things in your garage that could be used to pound in a nail. At the top of a ladder, rather than going all the way down to get my dropped hammer, I have tried screwdrivers, wrenches, pliers and even a belt buckle. Hammers work best.

We need tools, you and I—when broken down on the side of the highway, when standing at the top of the ladder or in the midst of a friend's mini-crisis. It's nice to have the right tools handy and the know-how to use them. We believe that having and knowing how to use tools for helping each other, really helping, should be a part of every believer's basic training—sort of "Friends 101."

God has specific tools for specific purposes. There seems to be a way to accomplish certain things in His Kingdom. There is a time for, and an approach to, every issue we face. The wrong approach will go nowhere. You cannot repent of a demon and you cannot cast out the flesh. Trying to help a friend before they are ready is like eating unripe fruit. You can do it, but it is not worth the effort.

Believe me, I've tried.

That is our first foundation about process:

FOUNDATION #9—

Apply God's solutions.

If God's solutions were hard or complex, then we would all be lost. In our experience, we find His solutions are few and simple, depend on honest, humble hearts, require that we listen to Him in the midst of ministry and rely on faith in His power and willingness to help us.

There are two key points I want to make about our tools before I introduce Sozo. Many of our tools, maybe all of them, involve speaking words; and many of our tools rely on intuition and perception and not on logic alone.

1. God is good, Satan is bad.
2. Your freedom is God's will.
3. We have hidden enemies.
4. Issues are not random.
5. There is always a reason.
6. Prisoners and captives.
7. Partners with God.
8. A culture of honor.
9. Apply God's solutions.
10. An event and a process.

Mere Words

At the outset it is important to grasp the fact that our words are powerful—when they are an expression of our heart's intent, our will, our agreement and our faith. For example, from God's perspective, if a young couple were to have sex even ten minutes prior to marriage, it would fall under God's proscriptions against fornication; and there would be negative consequences realized later on. However, ten minutes after the ceremony, God says, "Read the Song of Solomon for a few good ideas and go have fun with My blessing." What changed?

They spoke mere words. They stood in agreement. They made a vow. And everything was different. God says:[1]

> Death and life are in the power of the tongue, and those who love it will eat its fruit.
>
> Proverbs 18:21

Death and life are in the tongue's power. What are repentance, forgiveness, vows, lies, agreements, covenants and promises if not mere words? Words that, when spoken from the heart, are binding, powerful and life-changing. They have the power to create and tear down. They are the stuff of the Kingdom of God—and of the kingdom of darkness.

God says that He has given us specific weapons to destroy these binding strongholds and that from His perspective (the *only* one that matters) they are mighty. And they normally consist of "mere words." The literal translation of 2 Corinthians 10:3–5 is:

> For though we walk in the flesh, we do not war using soulish or fleshy weapons, for the weapons of our warfare are not of the flesh, but mighty through God for the demolition of strongly held places within us that we do not control. We are throwing down false speculation, imaginings and every high place that exalts itself against knowing God, and we are

taking every perception, thought and mental device captive and placing it into listening submission to Christ.

In this ministry one of the things we do is lead people to undo bad deals they have made and to vow to do better things, to forgive, to bless, to renounce. The power of some of the tools in subsequent chapters lies in their ability to put us in the emotional or revelational place where we are eager to make such godly and well-conceived statements. They gently open us up so we are more than ready to undo bad covenants we have made in the past. They assist us in being willing to draw on the ability to cancel debt owed through what Jesus has accomplished. Many of the techniques of this book are merely ways of framing our words to effectively vow before God and call on Him to enforce our vows against the kingdom of darkness.

Second, our tools are based on both rational thought and nonrational perceptions. The deepest motivations, wounds and constraints within us are largely nonrational and are often hard to access through logical questioning and reasoning. Even when we can explain our inner drives, we cannot always easily deal with them from the place of cognitive understanding. In the therapeutic world this seems to have led to the invention of many sometimes strange-sounding counseling techniques that try to get around the brain barriers (e.g., primal scream, transactional analysis, regression analysis, hypnosis, etc.).

Noted *Today Show* psychiatrist, Dr. Gail Saltz, in her book, *Becoming Real*, states:

> One of the reasons I have written this book is that in this day and age of advancing psychopharmacology and the various cognitive therapies, we have lost sight of the existence and the power of the unconscious. It's been a trend to focus on our chemistry or biology or on therapies that are about what's going on in our conscious mind and how we can alter them. I have nothing against these therapies—they

can be extremely useful—and I'm a believer in medication for the right people at the right time and under the right therapeutic conditions. But I also know how tremendously powerful the unconscious mind is. In some ways, it is more powerful than our conscious minds because we don't easily see the tendrils it shoots out and the stories it creates. We don't see how those stories make us think, behave, and feel in certain ways. When we dismiss or diminish the power of the unconscious, it is like operating with our hands tied behind our backs.[2]

She goes on to say that it is the stories we tell ourselves that drive our behavior—our internal dialog. In ministry partnered with God, we are often able to move quickly to these inner stories. Not only does God know the totality of the unconscious mind, He also knows the false stories (beliefs) we have told ourselves and were told and the key to unlock the prisons we are in. He can, in a moment, show us what direction to take, what to declare, what to speak and what to say. Often false beliefs were laid into us pictorially, and the surest way to replace them is to let God and the inner spirit of the person direct us—bring pictures, inner visions, stories.

The tools and approaches we use tend to be visual and often story- or memory-related. The instruction that does happen is in conjunction with these other approaches to help explain them, to bring biblical truth, to amplify what is felt or seen or to give practical application of something realized or experienced.

Road Map—Tool Summary

Here is a quick summary of the tools and a road map for the rest of the book, parts 2 and 3.

Part 2 (Getting Started) contains the basics of Sozo prior to learning the more advanced tools of part 3. It is a good place to start. I will introduce three basic concepts—WESUD, "Doing Kingdom Business" (DKB), and the Fruit Loop in chapter 7—and then put them together in chapter 8.

1. *WESUD*—We use WESUD as an organizing framework for ministry. It helps us see what kinds of things we might be dealing with: Wounding, Entanglements, Sin, Ungodly beliefs or Demons. When you sit down with someone, after you order your double latte, you are thinking, *WESUD—what are we dealing with here?*

2. *The Fruit Loop*—In a typical ministry session we use WESUD with a five-step process we call the "Fruit Loop" (this is a *fun* ministry, after all!). It is designed to keep us on track, and on time for dinner. For example, when we encounter someone who is hurting, we use the steps of the Fruit Loop to walk them through ministry. I'll give more details later, but for now the steps are Fruit, Root, Boot, Loot and Scoot.

3. *Doing Kingdom Business*—As you saw, within WESUD there are a number of actions we can take, such as forgiving, renouncing, repenting, declaring, etc. We call these actions "Doing Kingdom Business" (DKB). Renouncing is doing Kingdom business. Forgiving is doing Kingdom business. No action is the exclusive property of one of the WESUD buckets. For example, we might use granting forgiveness as part of our ministry for a wounding issue, entanglement issue, sin issue or ungodly belief issue. We use it whenever we need to.

In part 3 (More Advanced Tools), we have borrowed, modified and developed tools that accelerate and improve our ability to deal with the issues uncovered in WESUD. Some of the more common ones are discussed in this book:

DVD

1. *Dealing with Demons* (chapter 9)—Usually the demonic is commanded to leave as part of normal ministry, and there is little problem, no resistance and no
manifestation. It just happens. But when we encounter
the demonic in a way that demands more focused attention, we have a set of techniques and understandings to help us.

2. *The Four Doors* (chapter 10)—This tool is a way to
organize things for a thorough "spring cleaning." It
has as its primary focus probing key areas of sin that
show up in a person's life, finding the root(s) and dealing with them. It is a great thing to do once with a
couple of good friends—like getting a thorough physical exam.

3. *The Father Ladder* (chapter 11)—This tool has as its
primary focus the establishment or restoration of relationship with Father God, Jesus and the Holy Spirit
through dealing with earthly familial relationship issues and letting God bring a present revelatory picture
of Himself to the person.

4. *Presenting Jesus* (chapter 12)—The "Presenting Jesus"
tool is primarily focused on healing emotional wounding. It is based on the idea that we have been wounded
in the past, and our beliefs about that wounding have
an impact on our lives today. It is simple cognitive
therapy on steroids—Jesus does most of the revealing,
and logic takes a subservient, but important, role.

Process

You grow and change into the likeness of God over time.
If God were to tell you everything that needed transformation for you to be like Him, to live eternally with Him in
comfort (His, yours and your eternal neighbor's), you might
be discouraged.

But He knows He has time and He is in it for the long haul with each of us. He is committed. It is a natural and organic process—with a sure ending.

> For I am confident of this very thing, that He who began a good work in you will perfect it until the day of Christ Jesus. . . . Work out your salvation with fear and trembling; for it is God who is at work in you, both to will and to work for His good pleasure.
>
> Philippians 1:6; 2:12–13

God thinks you are okay and attractive to Him even while things are taking time.

We are all a little like a balloon rising naturally to its designed altitude. We are supernaturally intended to grow, expand, rise and mature. But each balloon is tied to the ground by one or more cords of different lengths. These cords are the constraints caused by the categories of issues framed in WESUD.

They limit us, stop our rise, keep us stunted and diminish our capacity for destiny fulfillment. We rise naturally until the shortest cord is stretched tight. Then we are caught up short—short of destiny, short of God-inspired desire. In God, the cords are rarely lack of talent or even opportunity—they are character based. A person may *rise* to great heights based on personal anointing, charisma and talent, but they will *stay* there only because of godly character. So it becomes a temporary ascendancy—our fifteen minutes of fame. Then we crash.

When a cord is cut, through Sozo ministry, we find we rise rapidly to the next point where we are again caught up short. God can change something in our lives in an instant. Freedom and relief can be immediate. Then we grow and consolidate the gains, changing our minds and habits in line with the new truth and freedom. Then we come up short again. Then we repeat the process. God calls it going "from glory to glory."[3] We call it our last foundation.

FOUNDATION #10—

An event and a process.

This is God's wonderful hand in your life. It is a sure thing in His eyes. We go along and something comes up. We deal with it in a godly way and keep going. We are caught up short by something else. If we see it as an opportunity for growth and change—for transformation—then we count the cost, pay the price, take the steps and move on.

1. God is good. Satan is bad.
2. Your freedom is God's will.
3. We have hidden enemies.
4. Issues are not random.
5. There is always a reason.
6. Prisoners and captives.
7. Partners with God.
8. A culture of honor.
9. Apply God's solutions.
10. An event and a process.

What would a church, a group of friends, a cell group, a family, a marriage, a . . . well, you get the picture—what would it look like if we all agreed that we would partner with each other in this wonderful ascendancy toward destiny, calling and righteous living? What would it feel like if I knew I could go, with confident assurance, to a friend or mate with my issue (or they could call me on something without my being defensive) and we could agree together to go after something that is attached to me—wounding, entanglement, sin, ungodly beliefs or demons? What would it feel like to be able to do so as a matter of course, as a matter of life, as a habit?

I am thinking it would be heaven on earth. I am thinking it would polish up that Bride and make her spotlessly presentable to her groom—our Jesus!

Getting Started

7

Key Elements

So [Jesus] said, "A nobleman went to a distant country to receive a kingdom for himself, and then return. And he called ten of his slaves, and gave them ten minas and said to them, 'Do business with this until I come back.'"

Luke 19:12–13

In theory, theory and practice are the same. In practice, they are not.

Albert Einstein

Reality is that which, when you stop believing in it, doesn't go away.

Phillip Dick

Never ruin an apology with an excuse.

Kimberly Johnson

A simple way to organize our thinking for first responder Sozo ministry is to consider (1) the kinds of issues we deal

107

with, (2) the typical steps we take to walk out freedom and healing and (3) specific actions we may take in the midst of the steps. As summarized in chapter 6, the kinds of issues are organized into "WESUD," the steps are arranged as the Fruit Loop and the specific actions we take all fit into "Doing Kingdom Business." Let's walk through these in that order, and in the next chapter put them together.

WESUD

I organize my thoughts in terms of "buckets." For years I took note of the kinds of issues I encountered in order to prepare a mental checklist of techniques and tools. It got long and convoluted. God has long since dealt with my insecurity in that area. He helped me see that He Himself had established categories to help our thinking and had a story to perfectly illustrate each one. And they are found together in Luke 15.

In Luke 15 God lays out the four principal ways we get in trouble, His part in them and especially the different techniques that are at the heart of each issue type. Luke 15 contains four parables: the lost coin, the lost sheep, the Prodigal Son and the older brother. When you think of these being different kinds of issues in a person's life, they come to nuanced life with layers of applications and understandings, of equal parts prisoner-and captive-based problems. If you read them you will see a set of actors, amazing parallels and subtle differences. You will see each member of the Trinity portrayed.

When we add the fact that we need to deal with demons on occasion, we find that nearly every issue we encounter can be placed in one of these categories. I use the acronym WESUD: *W*ounding, *E*ntanglement, *S*in, *U*ngodly beliefs and *D*emons.

Watch this.

The Lost Coin (Luke 15:8–10)—Wounding

The coin was lost through no fault of its own. In life coins might be lost for many reasons. Maybe it was considered worthless—dropped and never picked up again or missed; maybe it was neglected; maybe it was the victim of purposeful abuse. The act of being lost is traumatic to a lost coin and normally leaves a wound, memories, resulting scars and a warped interpretation of what happened that builds in the basic lies listed in chapter 4. Where the coin ends up when it is lost is a place that is dark, hidden and probably filthy or unclean. People just walk past, unwilling to stoop and pick it up. Maybe you can see yourself in this parable and bring your own description to what it means to be a lost coin.

God, as a woman (a gentle nurture, which is characteristic of the Holy Spirit), lights a lamp (brings revelation of truth), sweeps the house clean (removes the filth and pain), finds the coin and rejoices over it with friends and neighbors (restoration).

The primary ministry approach for a lost coin (wounding) is to *release* wound-based lies compassionately and gently. It is to (1) help the person define their pain and the lies they believe, (2) hear truth and release the lies, (3) grant forgiveness as appropriate and (4) bless.

The Lost Sheep (Luke 15:4–7)—Entanglement

The sheep wandered from the flock, perhaps through a combination of ignorance, naïve rebellion or enticed curiosity. It gets lost and for some reason cannot make its way back, perhaps entangled and ensnared as the old classic picture portrays. It is lost and confused; maybe it does not even know the danger that is prowling, "searching for someone to devour." It is easy prey for a passing wolf. God, as Good Shepherd (Jesus), knows the sheep is missing and places very great value on it. He leaves the rest and searches for the sheep, places it on His shoulders (takes the weight or guilt Himself without recrimination) and rejoices over it with friends and neighbors (restoration). Notice He does not blame or chastise the sheep; the entanglement itself did the teaching and warning.

Emotional-spiritual entanglements include ungodly soul ties, binding self-vows, false covenants and agreements with darkness, self and external curses, generational iniquity, unforgiveness and its consequences, dabbling in the dark side, etc. The primary ministry approach for a lost sheep (entanglement) is to (1) recognize the nature and source of the entanglement, (2) *renounce* it, (3) let Jesus take or bear it, (4) replace it with truth and a right agreement with God and (5) bless.

The Prodigal Son (Luke 15:11–24)—Sin

The Prodigal Son openly rebelled, lived in sin and suffered torment. He lost his perspective, his "senses." He went farther than he planned, stayed longer than he wanted, and it cost him more than he could afford. It ruined him. When he came to his senses, repented on the inside and took steps back home, his Father (God the Father) ran to him, kissed him, covered him (took away his shame), gave him a ring (a restored position as son) and sandals (restored destiny) and rejoiced over him with friends and neighbors (restoration).

The primary ministry approach for a Prodigal Son is to *repent* of sin, to (1) recognize the sin and come to an awareness about what it really is, (2) repent of it, (3) receive forgiveness and restoration and (4) bless.

The Older Brother (Luke 15:25–32)—Ungodly Beliefs

The older brother story did not get a parable of its own, perhaps because the ungodly beliefs he represents are a part of every story. But the older brother was unable to come into both intimate relationship with his Father and enjoyment of his inheritance because of his performance orientation.

[handwritten margin notes: Older bro: No intimacy w/ Father. No enjoy. of in-heritance. Performance]

He did not know the Father and believed things about Him that were false. The Father comes out to him, addressing the three main issues of ungodly belief: his false beliefs about his relationship to Papa God ("son"), his own lack of intimate relationship ("you have always been with me") and his inability to enjoy the inheritance ("all that I have is yours").[1] Then He invites him into the celebration (restoration) and loving fellowship within the family.

When we heal wounding, undo entanglements and repent of sin but still feel distant and unsatisfied, ungodly belief is almost always the reason. Our foundational sense of who Papa God is has been warped. Our foundational sense of what Jesus has done is incomplete. And our foundational sense of the moment-by-moment uplifting presence of the Holy Spirit is missing. The primary ministry approach for the false and ungodly beliefs of the older brother is to *reveal* truth, to (1) recognize the ungodly beliefs that interfere with relationship with God and ability to receive from Him, (2) get revelation about the truth, (3) repent, (4) declare the truth and (5) bless.

Demonic Issues

For completeness we also know that dealing with the demonic, either as a by-product of ministry or with overt focus, is part of most ministry sessions, and thus have added the demonic component to our acronym. As we illustrated earlier, demons hover over every other issue, adding energy and lies to make them stick and build them into a stronghold.

The primary ministry approach for the demonic is to *rebuke* and cast out, to (1) find the reasons the demonic is present, (2) remove those reasons, (3) assert authority over the demonic to remove it and (4) fill the place of demonic influence with truth and blessing.

Did you notice something each of the four parables had in common? Yes—a party at the end! God is into celebration, good food and intimate fun. *Rejoice* is just another word for "party." I like that. Make sure you rejoice.

Now on to the second component of our framework—the general steps, or road signs, we keep in mind in every first responder ministry situation.

The Fruit Loop

Driving through my small town is an exercise in solving the labyrinth. Even after many years of twists and turns, I love those signs in the middle of town with an arrow that say, "HWY 431." I am still on the right course. As mentioned previously, we have developed a simple five-phase process to do just that: keep you on track through the twists and turns of ministry.

It is called "The Fruit Loop." The steps do not have to be done sequentially; there is freedom and flexibility. Go with God, keeping an eye on the steps more for completeness. These steps may be initiated in any number of ways, most of them informal. The person may come with a problem, or it may be uncovered in conversation. A friend may initiate with another as part of bringing about reproof and loving restoration in their life.[2]

We are called on to simply deal with what is now presenting—"the fruit" or the thing God is after, and to bring truth, grace and compassion to that area. We are normally looking to identify the *stronghold*, the place inside that does not allow Jesus to be both intimate Friend and powerful Lord, so is leading to the current problem.

We do not have to try to untangle everything, only the thing God is after. Sometimes it is *the* lynchpin, releasing whole structures; sometimes it is the next peel of the onion, taking off a layer of lies, pain or unbelief. Remember process. Remember there is both sin and wounding. Let God clearly

112

identify and frame the issue(s) needing to be dealt with. Ask God to reveal to you what He is focusing on right now.

The steps are:

1. *Fruit*—"What is going on?" Current events, feelings, breakdowns, etc., are signposts that point to a deeper reality. Bringing definition to these opens the way to healing. The goal of fruit is to bring some WESUD definition to current events, to put a handle on them, but in a gentle and noncategorizing way.
2. *Root*—"Where did it come from and why?" We trace bad fruit back to a bad root. We drift back in time; we ask God to show us; we query the person about first occurrences, origins and reasons.
3. *Boot*—"Clear out the problems." We get rid of both the problem and the lies and dark energy that are helping to sustain it. We seek to fix what is broken, heal what is ill and undo what is binding the person.
4. *Loot*—"Take back what was stolen." God intends for our healing and restoration to cost Satan something. We look for God's intent in the situation both current and past, for God's destiny objective of blessing and for what has been stolen.
5. *Scoot*—"Make life choices and changes." We are practical. We make provision to walk out and defend the new ground that has been taken. We are realists and know that every victory is a product of both God's power and human will and desire. We identify steps, decisions and actions that should be taken to make the advance of the Kingdom permanent.

Doing Kingdom Business—Basic Concept

Now let's talk about the specific actions we take within a session, the third element of the overall framework. Recall earlier that we talked about "mere words." In this element called "Doing Kingdom Business" we are literally executing business in the Kingdom. We are taking advantage of the cause-and-effect reality of the world to cut off an old reality and initiate a new and godly one.

"Doing Kingdom Business" rests at the center of the Sozo technique and deals with identifying and reversing the "legal" side of WESUD.

It is a set of techniques or understandings based on the foundations and on the fact that we can, through Christ, stop the cycles of negative consequences of past and present actions, and set into motion cycles of blessing and freedom. It is not impersonal but a partnership with God within our lives.

The writer of Hebrews says it well:

> Let us also lay aside every encumbrance and the sin which so easily entangles us, and let us run with endurance the race that is set before us, fixing our eyes on Jesus, the author and perfecter of faith.
>
> Hebrews 12:1–2

Read that again *very* slowly. Lay aside. Every. Encumbrance and sin. Easy entanglements. Run and endure. Set race, fixed eyes. Jesus! Author. Perfecter.

Can you see yourself doing this?

How is this done? Through doing Kingdom business from the heart.

As stated in chapter 4, there is a legal, or perhaps supernatural, set of laws all revolving around the tendency of sowing and reaping. When these laws are broken, consequences result. Everything, good and bad, began somewhere. This can happen as a result of actions, decisions and choices: prior to becoming a Christian or afterward; others against us; past generations; even when in the womb. Adam and

Eve incurred a debt all of mankind is still paying on; apart from Christ there is no relief from it.

It would be nice if when we are saved everything negative just instantly disappeared. It could. We *are* new creations.[3] But it can take time and understanding to apply that salvation, that Sozo, to an area that keeps us from being who we and God know we really are. So it is applying the finished and totally complete work of Jesus to another part of our souls. We become partakers in the great exchange—His life for ours, His purity and rightness for our sin and wrongness, His peace for our anxiety and turmoil. It is finished; now we lay hold of it—glory to glory.

It is a good deal for us. No strings attached.

That is "Doing Kingdom Business" (DKB).

Leading Another through DKB

Part of doing Kingdom business is leading the person through steps to freedom via the Fruit Loop. In the midst of these steps we can do such Kingdom business things as: forgiving and removing judgment, confessing and repenting, submitting to God, declaring, breaking covenants or wrong ties, binding and loosing, casting out, releasing, claiming justice, reclaiming lost ground and assuming or coming under legitimate authority. We identify the issue in the Fruit step; understand its origin and nature in the Root step; undo it in the Boot step; restore what was taken in the Loot step; and help to protect it going forward in the Scoot step.

DKB is all about reversing the things that were done using our heartfelt words, spoken and believed. We often ask Jesus where we should go and what we should do.

We use "repeat-after-me" prayers to do so. Simple incantations and heartless, mindless repetitions are useless, or worse. People make real changes and legal contracts in the spiritual realm when they mean it. Thus we should never imply, "Repeat after me whether you agree or not."

A person may not know just what to say but that they really want to say *something*. The purpose of repeat-after-me prayers is to help the person to actually express real truth and not the half-truths we often hear prayed. We lead them effectively through this much like the wedding officiate leads the bride and groom through their vows. They mean it, but just need help with the words that express what they mean.

For example, in forgiveness we often hear something like, "Please help me to try to forgive so and so." That is not very effective. We can lead the person to express firmly real conviction and truth, and to speak reality, not pious religious phrases that skip across the surface of the heart rather than plunge deep into it.

For vow-breaking you might say, "Are you ready? Okay then, let's do a repeat-after-me declaration. Repeat after me an expression of breaking that vow, but feel free to say it better than I do if I don't get it quite right."

Repeat-after-me prayers can become God-led very fast. You begin with a simple prayer or declaration and find yourself moving quickly into Holy Spirit-led wording that touches the very core of the person and brings them to strong emotion and tears. It can be a powerful tool when we allow the Holy Spirit to flow through us. It can be a tool for "priming the pump" of reaching and releasing pain.

The display of strong emotions is not a necessary condition for freedom. They can even be a smoke screen for truth and getting to the core of issues. They should never be expected or manipulated. When they appear naturally and as a response to deep conviction or release, that is great. But making a choice from the heart by the active will of the person, with or without emotions backing it up, is most effective. The key is "from the heart."

On the other hand, the absence of emotion can be an indication that the ministry is not being effective or of some other blocking mechanism (defense mechanisms, fracture, etc.). While we never attempt to manipulate emotions, we do encourage individuals to look intently at what has happened to them or what they have done; to feel and even experience the results of it; and to let their natural emotions flow. A good cry or expression of long-repressed anger is normally very therapeutic. Take the time to let people grieve over lost lives, lost innocence, lost love, etc. Hold them or touch them appropriately and with permission (we practice safe touch). *Do not* interfere with emotional expression or seek to stifle it. But also do not let it rule the person and control the session.

Find the balance.

In the next chapter I will give brief illustrative phrases for most of the kinds of things we do in DKB. There are four that deserve more discussion and serve as the core of each of the key WESUD areas within the parables: forgiveness, disentanglement, repentance and obtaining revelation. We will look at "Dealing with Demons" in chapter 9.

Forgiving and Removing Judgment

Background

Many Scriptures confirm that unforgiveness is a major hindrance to freedom.[4] God and science agree that unforgiveness is like a glowering emotional cancer eating away well-being, pockmarking a person with painful symptoms and periodic flare-ups. It causes torment, hinders prayer, contributes to ill health, destroys relationships and organizations and causes long-standing regional hatred. In our experience, 90 percent of "prisoners" are in prison due to harbored unforgiveness.

Many movies understand this. For example, the diatribe by Captain Barbossa in *Pirates of the Caribbean: The Curse of the Black Pearl*—describing in anguished detail the curse placed on him and his men because they stole Aztec gold—gives voice and vision to the internal torment I have observed in those torn between the suffocating death of holding on to the desire for revenge and the rankling injustice of seeming to let the offended go scot-free. The scene in *The Return of the King* where Aragorn speaks forgiveness to the ghostly warriors who had betrayed his ancestors many years ago shows the amazing torrent of comfort that comes from forgiving. The warriors seem to fade into soothing eternal peace as a healing wind blows.

Symptoms of unforgiveness (fruit) include an internal sense of torment, hatred and dark energy; anxiety and drivenness; a heaviness of heart when seeing or thinking of the person who wronged us; rehearsed arguments and vengeance against them in our minds; or avoidance of them. If we see them in the department store, do we scoot down the women's apparel aisle? Unforgiveness begins to dominate our thoughts and spill over into other aspects of life.

Symptoms of corresponding judgment include feeling sluggish and without a sense of power, buoyancy and well-being; having unexplained nagging physical problems; having periods of despondency; lack of sound sleep; or feeling hindered and opposed in life situations.

Judgment may exist in our lives when we seem to be continually treated with judgment by others in various situations—and often that judgment follows a similar pattern.

The more advanced tool in chapter 10 gives more specifics about leading someone into forgiveness, but several points are worth mentioning in this context of doing Kingdom business. Forgiveness is all about debt, judgment and wounding. It is about canceling debt owed us, stopping our judgment of the person and their motives and being healed of the wounding that occurred.

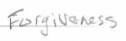

Forgiveness is saying that we release the person from whatever we might think they owe us and that we refuse to judge them anymore. We relinquish our rights for vengeance and retribution and turn them over to the Lord to deal with as He sees fit. Forgiveness may sound like, "You owed me love and protection. You did not give them to me. I forgive you that debt now."

Because we do not know what motivated that person, we also release any ways we judged them. Only God can execute judgment because only God is omniscient. When we forgive, we are saying we want to live and operate on the level of mercy and grace. If we demand justice against another, we may get it, but we will receive justice ourselves also, and justice for a sinner looks like torment. We give mercy and grace because we have received mercy and grace. We are saying we want what God wants for that person. We decide to forgive and give up our right to judge. In other words, "I give up my perceived right to judge you; only God knows your hidden reasons and motivations. I do not, and I repent now of judging."

Often when we gain God's perspective about the person, we find forgiveness less a decision of gritted teeth and more the natural outcome of love received from God and passed to another.

Every lost coin who has been wounded is eventually challenged by God to forgive the perpetrator—just like He did and still does. It is *not* easy to forgive in the face of pain and wounding, and there is no place for belittling the things that have happened. Forgiveness does not mean the person will allow the perpetrator free access to act against them again; it does not need to be followed by kind feelings toward the perpetrator; it does not mean that we excuse or ignore sinful actions by another. But it means we allow God to deal with the situation or person as He sees fit. It may sound like, "God, I ask You to show me Your love and truth in this area, to heal

Forgive from offended's perspective

How big Forgiving

my hurting heart. I ask for healing of my wounds inflicted by the other person and for help toward restoration."

When we are healed of wounds and gain God's perspective, forgiveness is easier, even natural. So we often deal with believed lies within a person's memory first. But sometimes, too, forgiveness is a *precondition* to freedom, and things do not progress until we forgive. God will tell us which way to go. Unforgiveness is often deeply rooted in lies we believe about ourselves, the person who did something against us and the circumstances. But God can supply truth and grace to carry us to the place of offering forgiveness, or choosing to forgive.

Forgiveness can involve repenting of judging God or having expectations, demands and beliefs about God that are untrue. It can mean forgiving ourselves, too—often we are our harshest critics. *No*

Ministry Step Tips

The speaking of forgiveness can be systematic or it can be used during the ministry process as areas of unforgiveness are encountered. It is often done using repeat-after-me statements. Sometimes the person is led to write down all the people he or she needs to forgive and what they have done.

Often it is much more effective if the person pictures the perpetrator and speaks as if they are addressing them: "_____, I forgive you for _____."

The things mentioned are not only actions the offending party took but can also be much deeper results or impacts such as, "I forgive you, _____, for teaching me the lie that _____."

Do not gloss over sin or allow the Sozoee to make up excuses. This is the time to call sin what it is and to really express the strong pain the person experienced—only then can we more fully allow the other one the mercy they need.

The following are some typical statements:

- "Lord, I thank You for forgiving me for my many failures and sins."
- "Lord, please grant me grace, power and a spirit of forgiveness. I choose to forgive now as I am forgiven."
- "I forgive _____ for _____, and I renounce any place I have judged them. I speak a blessing instead. I freely choose to release them completely now from the debt they owed me."
- "Lord, I repent of my judgment of _____ as if I knew all the reasons they did what they did. Please forgive me for taking Your place and role and for judging them. I ask You to forgive them and have mercy on them, and I ask You to release me now from judgment coming into my life."
- "Lord, I have placed expectations on You and judged You for not meeting them. I have set myself up to be disappointed in You. I confess that I do not understand sometimes but that I love You and want a restored relationship with You."
- "Lord, as I have forgiven others, I now receive Your unqualified forgiveness of my sins even up to seventy times seven each day. I confess with You that no sin is too great for You to forgive because of Jesus' sacrifice on the cross and His blood. I call His sacrifice good enough to cover my sins."
- "Papa God, because You have forgiven me I now choose to forgive myself of _____. I also release myself from accusation, judgments, self-slander and self-hatred. I accept myself for who I am and who You have made me to be."
- "Holy Spirit, I ask You to work holiness in me in this area and to change my heart, and to wash away from me the pain and wounding from this person and the

121

anger and resentment I have felt, and my desire for vengeance."

Go to deliverance as necessary. It may also be important for the minister to speak on behalf of all fathers and to repent to the person, "I just want to say, as a father (mother), that I am sorry that . . ."

Entanglements

I do not have to understand the inner workings of the gasoline engine to know that changing my oil is a good idea. I obey the manufacturer. I do not have to understand the intricacies of spiritual cause and effect to nullify dumb things and start doing smart things. I listen to God. Please review the key Scriptures in the endnote to receive insight.[5]

Entanglements come in many varieties:

- Past generations have committed or covenanted negatively (e.g., Masonic vows, cult memberships, family line curses, etc.).[6]
- My parents, or others in authority, have spoken over me words that limit or curse me even prenatally (e.g., "You're a mess," "You'll probably be just like your stupid grandfather," "You'll never get math").
- I unwittingly made agreements with the demonic for protection or some other perceived need (e.g., "If you keep me safe you can access me," "I need your anger to protect me").
- I have spoken self-limiting curses, contradictory to the Word of God, to myself in my head (e.g., "Bob, you're such an idiot," "I'll never be able to do it," "I'm just a sinner"). *yes*
- I have joined organizations or groups whose initiation rights (formal or informal) caused me to vow negatively

122

or swear idolatrous allegiance (e.g., fraternities, lodges, secret organizations).

- I have cursed and judged another, causing judgment *unjust* to come on me.
- In a fit of anger I have sworn to my own injury ("I'll never be like you," "I hate you").

Ministry Step Tips

When I am not sure what is happening, it is often a good idea to simply ask God if there is some kind of curse, vow or covenant that has been made. He is often willing to bring a thought or memory to mind just like He did for David concerning the Gibeonites, described in chapter 4. He may show us a past generation in a picture, a memory as a child, a relative, etc. Verification in some of these cases is not possible. But we do not need details or even verification to renounce what we have been shown. We trust God.

Once we recognize what we have seen, we frame it and lead the person through renouncing. Forgiveness and repentance may also be needed, as well as declarations of truth and replacing the false covenants or agreements with those provided by Jesus under the New Covenant.

Because Jesus bore the curses and bought our freedom, we can annul and renounce entanglements. Typical statements are included in the next chapter in the Boot step. Specific phrases will be given in the next chapter.

Sin Issues

Sin is not unimportant. It was so important God took care of it Himself. Sin must be confessed and repented of. It is (almost) that simple. Help the person realize that sin is never the issue with God. Jesus dealt with all those sins at the cross.[7] God is not mad at them. Sin does not damn them. And they are helpless to walk things out without God's grace.

123

They have true reconciliation with a Papa who sees them coming from far off and runs to cover them with a robe and give them a ring . . . and hold a party on their behalf.

Scripture is clear and unconditional.[8] Sin requires confession, repentance, cleansing and, if appropriate, deliverance. Confession says a person agrees with God's standard and estimate of their mind, heart and actions. Repentance, like forgiveness, flows naturally out of knowing God's perspective on the issue or situation—coming to "our senses."

God has a role in giving grace to hate sin and repent. Believers have a role in keeping themselves under that grace. Cleansing means allowing the blood of Christ to clean this particular area of their lives. Deliverance means taking authority over and casting out demons that entered a person because of the sin.

Habitual sin is often not the result of simple chosen or prolonged rebellion and disobedience. It can be rooted in trying to get temporary relief from some painful situation. In those cases repentance is important but not foundational. The person needs healing from wounding and truth in place of the lies to set them free.

Real repentance is not simple remorse and self-pity. It is seeing that we have hurt another deeply or have lowered and hurt ourselves, fully facing our sin and turning to God without excuse. It is confessing we are helpless to change and crying out for help. It is being willing to bear the consequences and to make restitution.[9] It is being willing to confess our part and let it go, even if another is contributory.

It is important for the Sozo minister to perceive whether or not the person understands they are forgiven. Many have lived in low level or background guilt and accusation so long that they find it hard to accept that the sin and guilt can be taken away that easily. When people confess, they need to hear they are forgiven and know release and acceptance. It is insufficient to say, "It's all right." It is not all right, but it *is* forgiven . . . forever. God has allowed us to minister reconciliation to people and to speak forgiveness to those confessing just as He would.[10]

Ministry Step Tips

The minister's role is to remove roadblocks to this revelation and point the person in the right direction. It is to help them see the unbelief that keeps them trapped in sin, and to find root causes of sinful behavior in lies believed, reactions to hurt, rebellion and pride, etc. It is important that the one confessing sin calls it what it is and does not gloss over it. For example, it was "sexual perversion," not a "mistake."

Sometimes there is a need to experientially visit the sin event(s), using the "Presenting Jesus" tool (see chapter 12), and ask Jesus to speak to the forgiveness issue (e.g., a woman who had an abortion hears and sees Jesus receiving her and setting her free from guilt and shame). There may be a need to renounce lies of accusation and bind and cast out demonic involvement and influence in the sin area. Pray for the cleansing blood of Jesus to wash away this sin according to 1 John 1:9, Ephesians 1:7 and Colossians 1:20. Ask the person to claim that cleansing and thank God for saving him or her from this sin and bringing him or her near to God. Go to deliverance as necessary.

The following are some typical statements:

- "Lord, I confess the sin of _____. I choose today to repent of this sin and to obey God in this area, and to come under Your Lordship in this area of my life."
- "Lord, I confess that I am helpless to change myself and humbly ask You to change me from the inside. I submit myself to You. I take _____ to the cross and ask You to put it to death."
- "I ask You, Jesus, to cleanse me with Your blood from the sin of _____."

125

Speak forgiveness to the person and release from the guilt of the sin and its shame. "I want you to know that God says when you confess He takes away the sin and that you are forgiven of _____ and your guilt is washed away. It is Papa God's will to cleanse you from all unrighteousness and sin and to make you know you are clean."

If the evil one brings up more past offenses, take them quickly to the cross and confess them—following these steps. If old memories crop up and cause guilt after a session, tell the person to agree quickly that they were sin and then move quickly to thanksgiving that they are covered and that God has shown such mercy.

Ungodly Beliefs

The term *ungodly beliefs* was popularized in inner healing circles by the Kylstras.[11] Their material is extensive on this subject. The term refers to any belief that does not align with God's truth—both the truth of His Word and the truth about His character and nature. Scripture abounds with examples and admonitions about what we believe.[12]

Ungodly beliefs are based on our perception of circumstances and our paradigms about God (in His three parts), others, ourselves and the world around us. You will recall in chapter 4 the discussion about core lies. These are a type of ungodly belief and form a distorted foundation on which to build others. In that chapter I described how these beliefs begin and grow, aided and abetted by the demonic.

Symptoms of ungodly beliefs often form the driver and backdrop against which people live their lives. They are the hidden motivator for all sorts of life circumstances and behaviors that are unfruitful and even idolatrous. The law of sowing and reaping, of belief and expectation, tend to work together in a negative way to bring about the negative—thus reinforcing the lies.

It is important to ask Jesus to help you trace this manifest fruit back to its hidden root(s). Dealing with behaviors or circumstances will only indirectly and weakly address the roots.

Key to healing is getting God's perspective on a belief, a situation or an event that caused a belief, etc. As such, if advanced tools are used, the "Presenting Jesus" tool in chapter 12 is good for beliefs about others and the world. The "Father Ladder" tool might be best for beliefs about God and myself.

Ministry Step Tips

Behaviors and circumstances in the Fruit step give an indication of ungodly beliefs. Ask Jesus to show and to frame what is really believed. Test this with the person: "How true does _____ sound to you?"

Once the issue is framed, go to the Root step to see where it came from. Sources can often be generational and cultural. A specific upbringing within a family and religious setting may have imprinted someone with an understanding of Papa, of the work of Jesus and of the ministry of the Holy Spirit that are far from the truth. Ask Jesus to show a memory, a symbol, etc. Go with what is presented. If nothing comes, simply skip to the next step without knowing the origin.

Frame what is true. This is often *already* spoken by God in His Word and not a simple fresh statement—though both apply, and a fresh word is usually powerful and intimate. Often asking Papa or Jesus to show specifically what is true will bring amazing and personal revelation.

The first key to framing the truth is understanding the unquenchable, unhindered and unconditional love of Papa God. If, while I was a terrible sinner, I was loved and drawn to Him, how much more now that I am a son or daughter does He love me with great affection? The second key is the amazing and comprehensive work of Jesus in dealing with our past sin, our current sin, the sin tendencies of the flesh, the unbearable accusation of the law and the dark one who uses it against us; in providing us with the power working within us to overcome; and in the promised outcome in eternity of a glorified body living in eternal bliss with Papa & Co. (not to mention the firstfruits of healing).

Then go to DKB to break, repent, renounce, etc. Declare what is true.

The Scoot step is important here. Back the truth up with Scriptures (no preaching) and give homework. It may be important to write it down for the Scoot step. It may take some mind transformation (neural restructuring, actually) to begin to walk in this truth automatically.

Ken's Story

Only yesterday I was with a man who, throughout the course of his life, had become unknowingly entangled in four or five things—all innocent, all deadly, all the plan of his enemy. Together they wove a web around him creating the familiar "double bind" in his life—"damned if I do, damned if I don't."

We led Ken to forgive a past teacher who set him back a year unjustly. He spoke release of judgment and felt instant relief from tension he did not even sense existed—till it was gone. He renounced participation in past occult practices and saw that it was designed to divert his deep spiritual sensitivity away from the godly spirit world and to build fear in him. He declared his readiness to renew and reengage the living God in real-time communication and communion. Jesus is his advocate. He was not abandoned and on his own to find his way through the world. He saw the lie of fear that had bound him to a strong intellect as a defense against the unknown and uncontrollable—and he broke his agreement with that dependency, declaring his dependence on Papa

God alone. Fruit-Root-Boot-Loot. Forty-five minutes. Scoot is coming—he is determined!

His wife told me later, "Whatever it is that you two did, sign me up! He is smiling and light."

This stuff works!

8

Putting It Together

Jesus was saying to those Jews who had believed Him, "If you continue in My word, then you are truly disciples of Mine; and you will know the truth, and the truth will make you free. . . . Truly, truly, I say to you, everyone who commits sin is the slave of sin. . . . So if the Son makes you free, you will be free indeed."

John 8:31–32, 34, 36

How few there are who have courage enough to own their faults, or resolution enough to mend them.

Benjamin Franklin

Everything should be made as simple as possible; but not simpler.

Albert Einstein

This chapter puts together WESUD, the Fruit Loop process and "Doing Kingdom Business." Remember: Never forget your partnership with God and to honor people.

The Snappy Diagram

The diagram on page 133 shows what the Fruit Loop and WESUD combination looks like. We engineers love diagrams! If you do not, skip it and go on to the description following. Realize that this chapter is comprehensive in the sense that it incorporates actions for each of the key aspects of WESUD. In any setting you may simply deal with, for example, Prodigal Son (sin) issues or lost sheep (entanglement) issues, and most of the activities illustrated in the rest of the diagram would not come into play at all. You would only track along that row.

Across the top of the diagram are the five steps, or phases, of the Fruit Loop. Down the side are the five buckets of WESUD. In the "Fruit" and "Boot" columns are typical symptoms and actions, respectively.

If we know the more advanced tools of part 3 of this book, then we may use one of them to quickly get to definition and resolution. The most typical ones when matched to WESUD would be the lost coin ("Presenting Jesus"), the lost sheep (the "Four Doors"), the Prodigal Son (the "Four Doors"), the older brother (the "Father Ladder"), and more overt demonic resistance ("Dealing with Demons"). "Doing Kingdom Business" (DKB) techniques and actions are used in all cases in the Boot and Loot steps.

Let me reiterate that many Sozo encounters are simply short but effective conversations in which only a snippet of the diagram—the approach—comes into play.

Walk-Through

This is comprehensive, covering all aspects of WESUD. You would only do a bit of this in any session, so don't be scared! Come expectantly. Listen spiritually for God/Jesus/the Holy Spirit's[1] voice. Do not be afraid to ask the person

Figure 7

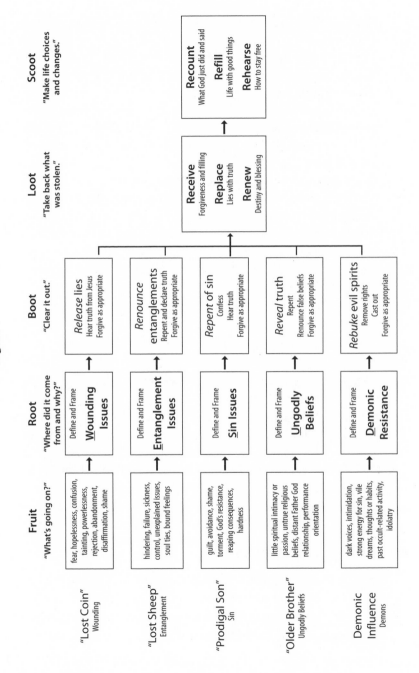

to close their eyes and to ask God direct questions. Speak encouragement and faith into them—this is their day.

The person in need is mostly just a "reporter" of what they are "seeing, sensing or hearing." They do not have to analyze, excuse, understand or interpret. They *can* hear Jesus speak inside them. There is no pressure and no wrong reports. We, as ministers, submit what we sense and see to the person and team as well. We make no pronouncements without allowing feedback.

Honor the person by giving them a voice. Let them talk. Listen to them and to God at the same time. Allow for naturally expressed emotion to be fully felt—wait. You don't need every detail. Do not let someone get into morbid self-analysis, religious babble, excuses or explanations letting themselves or others off the hook with misplaced mercy.

Find the balance.

Step 1—Fruit

In this step we are simply trying to discern and understand What Is Going On with them, or what transpired in a single event: "WIGO." It is all about listening with one ear toward the person and one ear toward God. It is important in this step to both hear what the person says, and also to think in terms of spiritual cause and effect and whether it is even an issue that you can or should deal with. Most often it is as simple as, "So, why are you here?"

We are trying to discern things like:

- What specifically is the person experiencing?
- What part of WESUD is involved?
- What is happening behind the scenes? What are the real motives?
- What is the stronghold area of sin and wounding? How should we define or name it? What does God call it?

- What lies does the person believe?
- Is this a pattern? What part of the issue lies with the person?

Necessary information in a ministry session can come from the person, inspired questions, a picture, word or sudden thought from God, a revelation offered and verified by a ministry team member and, rarely, from the demonic. Look at typical WESUD symptoms in the diagram for help.

Step 2—Root

In this step we are trying to understand where things came from, what is the source and origin of the issue, pain, etc. It is most often obvious—but always dig deeper than the surface. Often there is a more deeply rooted heart issue at stake.

It may be difficult to uncover, but it is always there. There may be a memory, picture or thought. Go with what is presented. God can work a miracle with anything. Sometimes the Sozo minister gets a picture or impression that later becomes a key for unlocking issues, or it becomes a road sign given at the right time within the Sozo. The root may be a time period, an event or a relationship. It may be found in generations past or in prenatal events.

If this is a simple cleaning up of an event, then this step is often skipped. For example, if you are just helping your child to forgive a classmate, then the event itself is the root and there is not a need to delve further.

We are looking for:

- What happened, when did it happen or where did it come from?

- What is the pattern? Is there a deep-seated false or unhelpful paradigm of life they hold about themselves, life, God, etc.?
- What door was opened during this event or the source event?
- Is the person experiencing the negative consequences of past sin or past pronouncements?
- What legal right, through words, actions or beliefs, did the devil have to control and try to destroy the person?
- What entanglement with darkness is the person in?
- What lies are involved? What biblical truth is violated or is applicable?
- Does the person hold unforgiveness and judgment?
- How did the person come into agreement with sin, wrong attitudes or ungodly beliefs?
- What destiny call is being targeted by Satan?

When you sense the need to look deeper, you might ask things like:

- "Jesus, what is the reason that _____?"
- "Jesus, where did I first come to believe the lie that _____?"
- "Jesus, what is this sin that I practice—will You help me name it honestly?"
- "Jesus, will you help _____ see the first time that _____?"
- "Jesus, what is the lie I believed about this situation that is false and harmful when _____ happened to me?"
- "Jesus, will You tell me what is true?"
- "Jesus, will You show me where You were when this happened? What do You think?"

Step 3—Boot

In this step we are cleaning out the problems. We can take the following key steps—matched to the five key areas of issues: *release* wound-based lies, *renounce* entanglements, *repent* of sin, *reveal* ungodly beliefs and *rebuke* demons. We go only to what is presented.

Release *wound-based lies by removing barriers to intimacy and trust of God.*

The person has been wounded and has formed self-protective barriers to keep safe from being hurt again. Unfortunately, in so doing they isolate themselves from Papa God as well. We may have been wounded during prenatal development when our spirits were tender and fully alive.[2]

It often helps to let the person remember what happened when they first learned to rely on a lying explanation for a situation and to ask Jesus to show them where He was when that happened and what He says is actually true about it, about this specific aspect of reality and life or about them. We need to hear truth and love and comfort—most effectively from God Himself.[3] This approach is formalized in the "Presenting Jesus" tool.

We must lead them to choose to allow those barriers to come down and to let Jesus in. If they have harbored unforgiveness and judgment, forgiveness needs to be spoken, debt toward another released and judgment of the person confessed and renounced.[4] They should be led to repent of any ongoing choice of self-protection, and admit and relinquish their reliance on lying explanations and understandings.

You might lead the person into praying things like:

- "Jesus, I confess today that when ____ happened I was deceived and wounded and did not know enough to allow You to heal and protect my heart."

- "Jesus, what is true about _____? Will You show me or tell me?"
- "I confess and declare now that when this happened I believed that _____ and today call it a lie and ask for freedom in this area. I reacted in self-protection and did not trust You or allow Your help."
- "I confess today those reactions and their present-day hold on me, and give them to You on the cross. I confess my need for You to help and save me."
- "I confess today my total reliance on You to heal my broken heart, and I ask You to forgive me and to cleanse me of all pain and hurt. I call on You, Jesus."

Renounce *entanglements and places of agreement with darkness.*

Our words have power to entangle.[5] Wrong and hurtful vows, covenants or associations need to be renounced, repented of and broken. Blessing can be given in its place.[6] Spoken curses, both by us and against us, need to be renounced and broken.[7] Soul ties, any illicit relationship in which one person puts another into control or bondage, need to be broken, and forgiveness and blessing spoken. Ancestors may have done something in the past that has been passed down to us. It can be negated and broken, forgiveness spoken and sin taken to the cross of Jesus.[8]

Take a stand against and renounce the places where lies have been believed, vows made, curses spoken, needed forgiveness harbored, etc., which opened doors to strongholds and demonic presence. Ask Jesus to show you if there is more you need to know. Follow the guidance from the previous chapter.

Help the person to declare things like:

- "I renounce my participation in _____ and break any agreement with it now."

- "I renounce my right to _____ and now give it to You, God."
- "I renounce the covenant made by my ancestors when_____."
- "I renounce the vow I spoke when _____ and take back any ground given."
- "I renounce the words I cursed myself with when I _____."
- "I break the covenant I made with evil when I _____."
- "I bind away from me now a spirit of _____, and choose to be bound to the Lord Jesus Christ."
- "I break my unrighteous soul tie with _____ and send back to her the part of her heart she gave me. I ask You to bless her and to heal her of her wounding caused by my sinful actions. I ask You, God, to return the part of my heart I gave to her and to heal me."
- "I declare my freedom from the lie of _____, according to Your Word."

Repent *of sin and rebellion.*

Our sin needs to be confessed, repented of and assigned to the cross. It is forgiven and covered by Jesus' blood and finished work.[9] The person must humble himself (or herself) and confess his sin, his part, his unforgiveness. He must not hold back or make excuses for himself or others. He should confess his part and actions, even if another was the major perpetrator. Make it simple, direct and clear.

You might lead the person into things like:

- "Jesus, today I confess the sin of _____. I repent of it now."
- "Jesus, I ask Your forgiveness for all the ways _____ has affected my life."

- "Jesus, I confess that that day I chose ____, but I repent of that choice today and I choose ____ instead."
- "I take _____ to the cross and ask You, Jesus, to put it to death."
- "I commit myself to breaking _____ out of my life, to turning from it and turning to Your ways."·

Reveal *ungodly beliefs*.

Help the person to see that they believe something—normally about God and themselves in relation to God—that is not true. This leads to beliefs, decisions, attitudes and other entanglements that establish barriers and distance between God and the person, leaving them lonely and vulnerable. The goal is to help them see both how untrue their beliefs are and how those beliefs have bound them and kept them away from God (Papa, Jesus, the Holy Spirit), who is the only source of help and comfort. The ungodly beliefs can be pinpointed quickly with the "Father Ladder" or "Presenting Jesus" tools. Believed lies need to be confessed, exposed and renounced. Truth should be confessed and declared in its place. We can declare allegiance to, and dependence on, Jesus.

You might lead the person to say things like:

- "I renounce my belief in the ungodly belief and lie of _____."
- "I repent of believing a lie and in living in accordance with it."
- "I declare the truth that _____."

Rebuke *the devil and his demons*.

We want to make sure we specifically identify places of agreement with, association with or bondage to demons, and break them. We discover most of these places through the initial steps, though God may give us more specifics here. Use your authority over demons and send them to where Jesus tells them to go. Use the fact of the power of the finished work of Jesus at the cross and His cleansing blood. You want to specifically name demons by function, activity or strongholds when possible.

Help the person to declare things like:

- "I rebuke, in Jesus' name and by His authority, every spirit of _____."
- "I rebuke the spirit that caused/deceived me into _____."
- "I rebuke any spirit that gained a foothold or place in me when _____."
- "I command you in Jesus' name to be silent and to leave me, _____."
- "I command you to go to the feet of Jesus, and to go where He sends you."
- "Lord, as a captive, I was unjustly _____ by the demonic and I ask You today for the justice due to me. I ask You to restore what has been stolen from me and to heal what has been wounded."

More on this in chapter 9.

Step 4—Loot

We want to take back what was stolen. We want the person to *know* that they are forgiven, cleansed and acceptable to God. We want them to be focused on God's destiny calling and on staying filled. We want them to feel good, both about what they have done and about God's unconditional love for them.

Receive *forgiveness and infilling from God.*

Ask God to cleanse the person in the specific places of sin and perversion, to return their focus to Him alone, to renew their love for Jesus and to turn their mind, will and emotions over to His control.

You might help the person to declare things like:

- "I now receive Your forgiveness for _____, Jesus, according to Your promise that if I confess my sins, You will forgive and cleanse me."
- "I agree with Your sacrifice for me on the cross and now receive Your washing with Your blood to clean me thoroughly from _____."
- "I thank You, God, that You will never bring up these sins again, that You have chosen to forget them because You love me so much."
- "I ask You to freshly fill me with Your Holy Spirit and with grace and joy, and I receive it now."
- "I ask You, God, to fill the empty, clean places with blessing, grace and righteousness."
- "I renew my devotion to You, Jesus, and come willingly under Your Lordship and protection."

Replace *lies with truth*.[10]

"You will know the truth and the truth will set you free" is a very real and practical concept.[11] Our goal is to help the person understand and declare what is true in areas they have believed lies and then to speak their allegiance to the truth. Lead them to declare their position under the authority of God's Kingdom in those areas and call on God for protection and strengthening. Speak scriptural truth in the areas of sin and wounding.

You might help the person to declare things like:

- "I declare and receive the truth that _____."
- "Jesus, I ask You to renew my thinking with Your truth about _____."

Declaring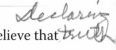

- "Today I choose to agree with God and to believe that *truth* _____."
- "I replace every lie and pattern of deception with truth in the area of _____."
- "I thank You, God, for Your love and care for me and rejoice in the truth that _____."
- "I receive Your love, Papa God, and I come willingly to You without fear that You will punish me. I ask You to speak to me of Your love and of my destiny. I receive the truth that You _____ (speak scriptural truth of the Father's love)."

Renew *joy, faith and hope, and refresh by ending with blessing.*

God has good things to say and He often uses people to say them. Make sure the person feels good about themselves, what God has done and how God feels about them (and they about God). Assure them that God will help them walk out the new freedom they have gained and assure them that some real transactions have taken place. Leave them with vision for the future by:

- Declaring what has been accomplished.
- Reiterating to the person Satan's plan and how God countered it out of His love for them.
- Declaring release of destiny and removal of hindrances.
- Speaking blessing and protection over the person.
- Asking God to give them faith and strength to walk out their new freedom.
- Insuring that they are feeling good about their relation with Papa God and that this event or issue has not clouded or darkened that relationship.

143

Let them know that they are not alone in this walk and that God began and will complete the good work in them. He is their partner and loves them totally.

Step Five—Scoot

This step is homework. It is walking out what has been revealed and experienced. It is helpful for the person to envision their lives, now cleaned out, with a chance to "re-decorate" the rooms that were cleansed. Instruct them to walk out what they have experienced in practical ways every day, and that they can use these same techniques every time they experience issues—they themselves can resist, confess, forgive, etc.

In this step we offer practical advice in three key areas.

Recount *with the person what transpired during the session.*

Help the person to list and understand what has been done. Help them to see what God clearly spoke to them—recount it for them. Lead them in thanksgiving and help them to *be thankful.* Write it down with them if necessary. Tell them to refer to what happened again and again—that it is a gift to them. Scoot these things into their lives.

Rehearse *with them what they can do if issues try to return.*

Show the person how to resist the evil one and avoid the temptation. Help them to see that they have the power to walk things out powerfully and a Helper to see them through. Scoot new thought patterns in their house, and scoot old ones out. We recite truth, watch our thoughts, keep encouraging company, focus our senses on good things and take advantage of the opportunity to walk free.

Refill *your life by replacing unhelpful behaviors and environments with renewed ones.*

Remember that Jesus said that the demonic comes back and, if it finds the room empty, will make it worse than before.[12] So choose to redecorate your empty rooms—first of all with God's presence, and then with good internal things, and then with good external things.

We are scooting things out that have tempted and harmed them. Help them to see the situations in which they have felt trapped or victimized and help them to choose renewed behaviors based on what they have been given during the session. Do not be deceived; bad company corrupts good morals. God said that one.[13] Flee youthful lusts. He said that one, too.[14] Help them to recognize situations, friends, practices, pastimes or environments that have led them into trouble and to scoot these out of their lives permanently. To draw a line not to cross. To work out their salvation (Sozo) with fear and trembling.[15]

Help them also scoot things in that will make for continued healing: good relationships, habits of prayer and Bible study, meditation on truth, habits of joy and thankfulness.

Examples

Here are a few abbreviated examples to illustrate the use of the simple steps above.

Mary

Fruit—Mary was estranged from her daughter despite attempts to contact her. They had not spoken in three years.

Root—We never blame the other one even if they are 95 percent of the problem. We can only deal with the person before us. So we did. When we asked Jesus to show Mary what was going on with her, not her daughter, it became clear in an inner picture that Mary still held strong negative opinions about her daughter—judgment. She also realized that it was her own sense of insecurity that was driving things from her end. She realized she was insecure about being a good mother and looked to the relationship to affirm her abilities—this points to a deeper place of wounding.

Boot—Mary knew she had forgiven her daughter before but stepped into it again and during a repeat-after-me prayer, things got really deep really fast. This time she also renounced the ways she continued to hold her in judgment. She confessed her motives were wrong. She asked Jesus to show her the source of her insecurities and eventually forgave her own mother for acting in the same way. She was able to release her insecurities as Jesus spoke comfort to her, telling her that she was very capable and that He was *more* capable. She could rest in that truth and just be herself—that was all her daughter really needed anyway. Lots of tears.

Loot—She accepted God's estimate of her and thanked Him. She listened to God's words of blessing and affirmation spoken over her own life. She then, in turn, spoke a strong and teary blessing over her daughter, speaking out what her godly dreams were for her.

Scoot—She stayed open to her daughter and maintained an attitude of blessing without control. She sent her an email when she felt prompted, just blessing her. She heard from her daughter in a surprisingly short time:

"Hey, Mom, want to have lunch? I have a surprise for you."

And, out of the overflow of her now-filled heart, she was able to bless her daughter without reservation, bring about restoration of the relationship and step into the role of trusted and wonderful granny to her new granddaughter.

Terry

Fruit—Terry was a young boy who, uncharacteristically, lashed out at a playmate. His mother saw it and asked him about it shortly thereafter—in private. Private is *always* good.

Root—After a little probing and asking where the ugly words came from and what was hurting inside, Terry talked about feeling rejected by some older boys on the playground who (from Terry's perspective) had not let him play. His mother, with reliance on Jesus, led Terry to understand that there may have been another interpretation of that and that Terry, although a big boy, was several years younger than those boys.

Boot—Terry forgave the boys for not being sensitive to his feelings and renounced his belief in his own rejection. He confessed his own pain and gave it to Jesus, receiving comfort in return. He repented of lashing out at the other boy and agreed to go to the boy and ask him to forgive him the next day. A spirit of rejection was told to leave Terry's presence, and Terry asked God to help him see that angels were walking with him.[16]

Loot—Terry was led to understand that his feeling of wanting to be in the middle of things was a gift of God and that he was a leader. He was encouraged that he was one who could give support to others and that what happened was the evil one's attempt to knock him off course.

Scoot—Terry received these words and announced to his mother that he was ready to go play. Off he went, happy and singing, no hardness able to form in his tender heart. He went to the other boy and asked to be forgiven. He even had to help the boy speak it. They became fast friends as a result, and five years later it is still a habit in the boy's life—keeping short accounts.

Ivan

Fruit—Ivan was a young man who was adrift in life without purpose or vision. He had little self-awareness and drive toward any sort of career or direction. He also had ADD.

Root—After asking about things in life without real result, Ivan was asked about the circumstances of his birth. He stated that his parents had been in the midst of divorce and that he was an unexpected and unwanted surprise. They stayed together for his sake until he was two, but it was tumultuous and stressful for his mother throughout the pregnancy.

Boot—Ivan was led to forgive his parents for bringing him into a world that, even in the womb, felt unwelcome and fear-filled. He was led to understand that God had a purpose for him despite the circumstances of his conception—he was not a mistake. We told spirits of deception who had stolen from him that it was their turn to be looted.

Loot—He declared that he accepted his purpose, that he would find it with the help of Jesus and that he fully embraced God's plans for his life and for his living. He was blessed by his friends. When he asked Jesus to show him where He was at Ivan's birth, he got a vivid picture of angels rejoicing and of Jesus smiling and nodding and saying, "Finally—presenting *Ivan!*" He cried and shook.

Scoot—He began to fill his mind with the truth about his destiny and began to look for God's hand in his daily activity. In short order, he began to feel drawn to commercial art, entered a trade school and was a class leader. Amazingly, his ADD began to wane and eventually disappeared. He is now the owner of a successful commercial art firm, a leader in his small suburban community and a big brother to several young men.

Tony

Fruit—Tony was having trouble with pornography. When probed it was quickly discovered that he was addicted to masturbation.

Root—When asked what he felt just before he decided to turn on the computer as a way to gain relief, he stated he felt

148

a deep inner loneliness and boredom. When God was asked why Tony felt lonely, Tony was shown an inner picture of his father walking away from him. God showed him a specific symbolic or representative memory of a deep feeling of abandonment and rejection because Tony was not interested in his father's cherished pastime. He also was shown the first time he turned to masturbation as a tool of escape—having been shown how to do it by another boy in the neighbor's garage using lingerie pictures in women's magazines.

Boot—Tony chose to forgive his father and, when he spoke release of the debt of love and affirmation his father owed him, God showed him a picture of his father's own loneliness and his father's dreams that he and his son would connect around this pastime. He saw his father's own inability to relate growing out of his own treatment as a boy. He wept and released ways he had judged his own father.

He renounced his choice of masturbation as an escape and chose to give his pain to Jesus on the cross—to be cleansed by His blood of all sin. He renounced his own agreement with pornography and spoke blessing to the women he had viewed, renouncing his agreement with the objectification of women on the Internet. He forgave the boy who taught him to masturbate and asked Jesus to show him a better way to walk out his pain. We cast out unclean spirits of lust and perversity. We told rejection it was rejected in favor of Papa God.

Loot—He turned to Papa God for comfort and affirmation. In the end he asked Jesus, with whom he felt very close, to show him a true picture of Papa God, to take him there. An amazing inner event happened wherein he was taken into a garden and ended up in Papa's lap looking into His eyes. Everyone wept then!

Scoot—He agreed to find another man with whom he could learn to walk fully free of this physically and emotionally addictive habit and to put controls on his computer. We recommended a book for him to read as well.[17] He agreed to flee youthful lusts.[18] Leaving the pain behind, he learned habits of self-control, met and honorably courted a young woman and is now happily married.

Sheri[19]

Fruit—Sheri and Roger were going down the road in their truck and hit a pothole. Sheri yelled, "Watch out, oh no!" There was an embarrassing silence when Roger said, "So . . . what's that all about?" It was too late. Sheri and Jesus were already way down the road. Roger was just along for the ride.

Root—Sheri's parents, in the past, made everything a big deal, going from zero to worst case in scant moments. Hitting a pothole would mean they would have to fix the truck, which meant they wouldn't have enough money for the mortgage, which meant they would lose the farm and everyone would die.

Boot—She renounced her agreement with that lie and that way of thinking and forgave her parents for passing this along. She asked Jesus what was true and received an answer about His faithfulness that deeply comforted and freed her. Memories of His care for her flashed into her mind. She was convinced.

Loot—She declared her singular allegiance to and belief in this great Protector and asked Him to take back every place where she had shrunk back from risk out of fear. She declared that God had not given her a spirit of fear but of power, love and a sound mind.[20]

Scoot—She looked at Roger and told him, "It's okay, Honey; it's better now, you can just drive." And like most husbands, he was both a little oblivious and deeply thankful to Papa for providing him with such an amazing wife. Three minutes was all it took.

Your turn!

Try it out. Walk through the Fruit Loop with your own issues. Walk through it with a friend. See if God is not faithful to you. And when you are ready to learn more, go on to part 3.

*More
Advanced
Tools*

9

Dealing with Demons

One Almighty is more than many mighties. All these mighty sins and devils make not one almighty sin or an almighty devil.

William Gurnall

Finally, be strong in the Lord and in the strength of His might. Put on the full armor of God, so that you will be able to stand firm against the schemes of the devil . . . so that no advantage would be taken of us by Satan, for we are not ignorant of his schemes.

Paul in Ephesians 6:10–11 and 2 Corinthians 2:11

Behold, I have given you authority to tread on serpents and scorpions, and over all the power of the enemy, and nothing will injure you.

Jesus in Luke 10:19

There are many treatises on demonology.[1]
This is not one of them.

Rather, this is just a practical look at how we encounter our enemy, why we can send him away and how we do so. This is a long chapter, and it leaves a lot out still. But it is a good introduction for first responders. It gives a framework in which you can place all sorts of follow-up understanding and knowledge. There is more, and after you feel comfortable as a first responder, I encourage you to go on to explore.

"Dealing with Demons" (DWD) consists of identifying, as necessary, the demonic presence in and around us, eliminating its right to be there and, under the authority of Christ, casting it out.

But first let me make a clear point.

Nobody gets to be Buffy.

We are after God, not demons. We are not focused on dealing with our "stuff," not escaping pain, not fixing ourselves. We are not all about fixing someone else—even if they *need* fixing. Passionate, intimate love from and for God is the main thing. Finding freedom from our emotional constraints and being rid of demonic influence is an *outcome* of relationship with God, not the focus of it.

Okay.

In a Sozo ministry session, it is often not necessary to use DWD if there is little or no perceived demonic interference. Most often demons simply go when commanded with minor or no manifestation as part of the Boot step in the Fruit Loop.

But sometimes freedom is impossible without dealing directly with the demonic. We cannot simply tell someone to control themselves or counsel them out of an issue if there is demonic influence and presence keeping things locked up and energized. Sometimes demons may want to hinder what is going on, subvert our attempts at freedom or challenge our authority to send them away.

We need another tool to do those things—that is what DWD is.

So . . .

If and when we turn to the DWD techniques, our basic questions are, "Why is the demonic (still) here?" and "What makes it think it can stay?"

Find and deal with the answers to those questions and you are most of the way there.

Stats on Our Enemy

In chapter 3 we saw that our enemy has hidden ways that specifically target our destiny call. Let us now go further and more applied.

This age and this world is, in a real sense, a war zone in which there are real casualties, prisoners, captives, destruction and loss. While Satan and his demons have been soundly and totally defeated (more on that later), there is still a struggle against his schemes, lies and handiwork in places of entanglement, sin and wounding. There are relatively few Christians who are not targets of, or vulnerable to, demonic attack or influence. Even with Jesus, Satan was only temporarily put off and awaited a more opportune time.[2]

Paul the apostle makes it clear as clear can be:

> For our struggle is not against flesh and blood, but against the rulers, against the powers, against the world forces of this darkness, against the spiritual forces of wickedness in the heavenly places.
>
> Ephesians 6:12

The spiritual "struggle" Paul talks about indicates a wrestling match in which one or the other is thrown down and pinned.[3] It seems to take place on many levels, but for convenience I will boil it down to only two: (1) *individual* temptation and trial from without, or individual demonic strongholds formed within, and (2) *external*, regional, territorial and institutional strongholds within societies, people groups, organizations, nations and geographical areas. We are focusing on the most common individual, hand-to-hand types of situations, though we may deal with the results of the other in an individual's life.

Demons take advantage of human weakness in our mental-emotional-physical "machinery." They attack and pervert human personality and attitude, emotions, minds and thought patterns, physical appetites and drives (e.g., hunger or sex). They seem to lodge in, or target, certain parts of the personality—especially *wounded* personality— with a particular assignment. Their two primary tools are accusation and deception.[4] You are deceived into believing lies or into sinning and then accused of being a failure and a sinner. Vicious cycle.

They entice, harass, torture, torment, compel, control, enslave, defile, shame, deceive, drive, trick, blind, dull, manipulate, dominate, bully, intimidate, accuse, influence, cause sickness and infirmity, tempt and help cause addictions. They can be the instruments of the dark side of the law of sowing and reaping. They enforce vows, curses, pledges and dark covenants. They warp natural urges and drives and force them to extremes. They are "religious" and love to invent doctrine.[5] They love uncontrolled flesh and fallen human nature. They steal, kill and destroy.[6]

Demons are liars and, unless confronted by God's authority, will always speak lies.[7] When commanded with legitimate authority (by Jesus and His followers) they tell the truth, though they will take advantage of every legal loophole not to do so or to get what they want.[8] Even when they tell the truth, its purpose is to avoid accountability, deceive or cause trouble.[9]

Many demons seem to have a particular "specialty" and need the help of others to more fully control a human personality. They can operate with a hierarchy (e.g., the "seven other spirits more wicked than itself" in Matthew 12:45, "Legion" in Mark 5:9 and the seven demons in Mary

Magdalene in Mark 16:9). There are certainly orders and differing powers, perhaps reflecting the different orders of angels from traditional Jewish thought. They are mutually cutthroat.

In the Bible, the titles given to some evil spirits are jealousy, evil, lying, perverse, sleep, heaviness, unclean, ignorance, harlotry, mute, deaf, infirmity, divination, deceiving, fear and error. These names are examples—not limitations. In reality, we have encountered many names, often surprising, many boastful. These names can give a characteristic and a "handle"—they indicate function or focus. It is not certain that they are all fallen angels.[10] But if they are, then, like angels, they may have other proper demonic or angelic names, too (e.g., Molec, Abaddon, Lucifer).

At higher levels they influence and control both physical places and the social structures of men: buildings, cities, regions, nations, institutions, organizations, governments and cultures. Within such institutional frameworks or families they can pass from generation to generation, maintaining their hold father to son, grandfather to grandchild. They can also somehow attach to or hide behind objects, whether idols or cursed things.[11]

Demons need a deceived host in which to most fully express their evil intent from the inside. They will even choose pigs over nothing.[12]

Authority and You

If all this feels a little disconcerting or otherworldly, that is normal. This section is for you. Read it several times, look up the verses and meditate on them.

I mean it!

Lawbreakers respond to authority, not to more laws. History can be seen as a contest for authority, won by God (like there was any question). In summary:

1. God gave Adam a measure of authority over the earth (Genesis 1:26).

2. Eve, through deception, and Adam, through rebellion, gave Satan their authority and subjected all mankind to demonic control (Luke 4:6; Romans 5:12–14; Ephesians 2:1–2; 2 Corinthians 4:3–4; 1 John 5:19).

3. Satan offered his authority to Jesus in exchange for worship of Satan. Jesus declined (Luke 4:7).

4. Jesus, while on earth, demonstrated what a righteous man rightly related to God can do, and He gave of His personal power and representative authority to the Twelve and the seventy (Luke 9:1; 10:17–19).

5. Jesus died in our place, took our punishment on the cross and was given all authority (Matthew 28:18).

6. When He rose and ascended, He totally and completely disgraced Satan and all his demons, annihilating their authority over any child of God (Colossians 2:13–15; Hebrews 2:14; 1 John 3:8).

7. Those who belong to Jesus come out from under Satan's authority, influence and control, move into God's domain and are given the "Greater One" within (Romans 8:37–39; Colossians 1:13; 1 John 4:4; 5:18).

8. Every child of God is seated with Jesus far above all demonic authority. We have derivative authority and fullness of the Spirit from Jesus to enforce His victory against our enemy (Acts 19:15; Ephesians 1:3, 20–22; 2:4–6; Colossians 2:9–10).

9. Jesus' Church is to *attack* the gates (place of authority) of hell and to prevail. We are to bind and loose according to the pattern, force and decisions we see in heaven, where there is *no* demonic authority or control. We bind what has been bound, loose what has been loosed, joining God's will and man's action (Matthew 16:17–19; 18:18–20).

10. When we go after the demonic, we bind it and force it out—this is violent, complete and forceful—even as it

7 sons of Sceva tried to cast out demons, but couldn't because not connected to JC - Demons had heard of Paul & knew JC.

Dealing with Demons

is gentle and loving to the person involved (Matthew 12:28–29; Mark 3:27; Luke 10:19; 11:21–22).

11. When Jesus returns He will visibly establish His authority and reign over the earth (Revelation 21:3–4).

12. The inevitable, final and eternal place for the devil and his demons is in the lake of fire, while our assured place is to reign with Jesus (Ephesians 1:7–10; 2:7; Revelation 20:10).

Everything changed at the cross.

Since the death and resurrection of Jesus and forevermore, Satan and every demon is in a state of utter defeat. That defeat is to be enforced on earth, as it is in heaven. Demons still work for control in the sons of disobedience and within the unaware Christian, but *must* respond to the authority and power of Christ and His brothers and sisters. Their ploy is to try to bluff their way out of compliance.

We *have* authority and *grow* in our realization, experience and exercise of it. There is no substitute for knowing on which foundation you firmly stand. We are not peers of or subject to demons. And it is not about our performance or perfection, which was nailed to the cross without our participation, but about the fact that we are hidden in and seated with Jesus. Remember, the most demonized person in the Bible, the Gerasene man, filled with a legion of demons, could not be kept from running and falling down at Jesus' feet.[13]

This authority given to believers is not some mantra or set of incantations, but is a living, relational and revelational reality. The seven sons of Sceva tried to cast out demons using such a secondhand incantation approach and suffered for it. The demons knew Jesus and had heard of Paul but knew these sons were not connected with that authority (Acts 19:13–16).[14]

How do we apply and enforce the victory won by Jesus? In the next sections we will talk about the typical encounters and actions we take with the foundational understandings we have.

Handling the Demonic during Ministry

Demons need something to work with, to feed on—pain or sin, wounding or guilt. Flies swarm because of, well, because of doo-doo.[15] Demons are like those flies. In this kind of ministry, we are after life's doo-doo and, secondarily, the demonic. The fly problem often seems to take care of itself when the doo-doo is cleaned up. We always check, and when we find we need to go after flies, we do. But flies are not often the point.

In most ministry sessions, we do not encounter demons' *presence* but we always encounter their *handiwork*. They may not be present *within* someone, but we have come to see that they seem to always be involved in schemes, snares, lies and attacks.

Step one is recognizing the demonic dynamic. How does it "look" or "manifest"? A manifestation is simply the visible evidence of a deeper, though heretofore hidden, reality. This has two aspects: how does it look in everyday life, and how does it look in a ministry situation?

Let us talk about the "ministry situation" version of manifestation first, as it applies throughout all the steps of the Fruit Loop. Then we will discuss recognizing the demonic in daily life as a part of the Fruit step.

Dealing with demons in an overt way is not uncommon in our ministry practice but certainly does not happen most of the time. The discussion here is for the situation we encounter when a demon manifests. It is not avoided nor sought. But if demons stand in the way of a child of God's freedom, they have to go—no question. If they are hiding, we smoke them out.

160

Demons will remain hidden until we get to their "food source"—the inner lies, entanglements, sin and wounding upon which they feed and hold; until something stirs them to react; or until they feel they have enough power to be hard to dislodge. Then they will make efforts to fend us off, scare us, resist, show off and threaten.

Demonic manifestations are neither good nor bad in themselves. It is the end result that matters. Often the way demons show themselves gives away their strategy or tactic for operating and reason(s) for staying. So a manifestation can be a good thing—but it is always a thing we bring under control. As a friend once said, "I don't care if they show themselves; I just want to know if they are coming or going."

Manifestations can look like a number of things internal *signs* and external: confusion, blank inside, dark feelings, sudden thoughts, crying, shaking, screaming, nausea, blank stare, yawning, sudden dark emotions (e.g., anger, despondency, *twitching* etc.), dulling of the eyes, contortions, facial change, a voice change, change in the "feel" of the room, false leads, a false inner picture of Jesus, inner dark voices, guilty or shameful feelings, physical infirmity (headache, sleepiness, coughing, retching) or emergence of a non-alter personality.

It may not be demonic at all!

If we encounter something that gives us pause, we simply pay attention and seek clarification. We will know—in God's time. But we *never* prematurely assume nor overtly accuse someone of having a demon. The Sozoee is not evil for having been victimized, and what has happened to them is not unusual.

Remember to honor the person. Make sure they know these things.

Manifestations have three sources—the Holy Spirit, demonic spirits and a frail human's honest emotions. We react by (1) following the Holy Spirit, if it is God, (2) expelling, binding and dealing with demons, or (3) understanding, helping, comforting and, as necessary, urging the person to exercise discipline if it is flesh. Fear may simply be just that—the person (or part of the person) being afraid of what is happening. Look for nondemonic reasons first. Realize there is always a mixture as both the human and the demon make use of the internal human emotional-mental-physical machinery.

We go by the Lord's timing, not that of a demon or even of the person. We do not swing at every pitch. At any time, if a person "manifests" a demonic presence and begins to lose control:

• Ask what's going on inside of them.
• Address the person with love and kindness; do not incite fear.
• Address demons and bind them in Jesus' name; order them to stop. Tell them that if they refuse they will be referred to Jesus.[16]
• Address the demon if it is time to cast out or make the person regain consciousness or control over themselves.
• Tell the person to take control over their body and mind and to open their eyes in Jesus' name. Help them.

Let's also talk referral.

The longer, deeper or more traumatic the demonization, the greater the ability of the demon to take control of the person's thoughts, emotions and even their body.

Because of its volunteer, relational, single-session (or a couple of sessions), "first responder" nature, Sozo practitioners are not equipped to deal with every situation and should not feel bad about recognizing when referral is necessary. That is a good and necessary part of being first responders—and friends.

If we sense we are really in over our heads (for example, the Sozoee is a victim of deeper abuse, exhibits dissociation, becomes physically threatening or violent as in more extreme manifestation cases), we bring comfort and encouragement, shut the Sozo down gracefully and work toward later referral to someone more skilled and experienced in dealing with these cases. Even the disciples referred a case to Jesus.[17] Always go slowly and gently in this arena. It is no place for bravado or foolhardy experimentation.[18]

What about you?

Sozo ministry often brings things to light in the Sozo minister. You yourself may experience confusion, emotions, blockage or sudden vile thoughts. First of all, vile thoughts or temptations are not sin—they are attacks to put us off. Even Jesus was tempted in "all ways."[19] God and you, not the devil, determine the timing of your own ministry. Normally, the things triggered in the Sozo minister are dealt with after the session with the help of the others there, or later. Not being perfect does not disqualify you to minister freedom. Rebellion does, and you are not rebellious.

Okay, back to a typical session in which DWD is used.

Starting a Session

Generally, at the beginning of more formal ministry sessions, we gently but firmly assert spiritual authority. The person may not even be aware of what we are doing or may not be sure they even believe in demons. Most will accept a simple, gentle and calm explanation or simply agree with our prayer or declarations. Once we are sure the person is comfortable and ready to go for it, if we sense demonic resistance or a need to, we may take authority over the session and bind away any hindrances to what we are about to do. We might say something like this (remember, no formulas or mantras!):

> "I command any spirit that does not name the Lord Jesus Christ, who died for _____'s sins, and does not bow the knee to Jesus to come to attention."

"I bind you now from hindering, blocking or in any other way stopping the work of God within this person now."

- "You may speak only if and when spoken to, or may say only what the Lord Jesus Christ gives you to say."
- "I ask You, Lord Jesus Christ, to send Your angels to enforce this command and to enforce compliance. Jesus, our reliance is on You and on Your authority within us according to Your shed blood and Your defeat of Satan and all his demons at the cross."

As we begin working through the "Fruit Loop," we come to realize we may need to turn to DWD at some point in the session and encounter the demonic more directly. Let us walk through the steps and show how DWD techniques can come into play in each of them.

Fruit Step—What's Going on Raises Flags

Okay. Let's talk about the "in everyday life" part of manifestation now. We are with our friend Bob.[20]

"So, Bob, what's going on?"

As Bob talks about his everyday life we become increasingly aware that there may be some stronger than normal demonic involvement and that the DWD approach may be good. How do we know that?

There are many ways demons find to manifest their insidious plans for destruction and control. Many people who are influenced or intermittently controlled are simply unaware of it. They may consider a certain sin, entanglement or wounding as part of a lifestyle. It feels like a hindrance or handicap, but a familiar one. Because of the culture or milieu in which they were raised or to which they have become accustomed, people may also be oblivious to the fact that a certain lifestyle, practice or belief is, in fact, sinful.

Demonic presence may often appear as an *exaggerated* and *energized* place of sin or lack of self-control. Below is a brief list designed simply to expand your thinking about manifestations. No single item on this list, in itself, indicates demonic activity, just as no one physical symptom always indicates a certain disease. But these items do raise suspicion (though you are not to be suspicious!). Many of these things are also deeds of the flesh—recall there is often a combination. Sometimes it is the exaggeration of the manifestation that is a clue. But that exaggeration can also simply be a result of pent-up emotions and anger released by seemingly small events.

Someone strongly influenced by the demonic may chronically experience or exhibit:

- Addictions
- Anorexia and bulimia
- Behavioral extremes
- Bitterness and unforgiveness
- Compulsive behavior
- Dark thoughts and impulses
- Deceitful personality
- Depression
- Emotional disturbance or long-term unbalanced emotions
- Escapism and withdrawal
- Extreme or exaggerated denominationalism
- Extreme self-focus
- False concept of Scripture
- False gifts of the Spirit
- False philosophical concepts, universalism
- False religion and belief
- Fears and phobias
- Guilt and condemnation
- Hearing internal or external voices
- Hereditary illness or chronic or repeated sicknesses
- Immaturity in character or relationships
- Irrational behavior
- Legalism or deep spiritual bondage
- Nightmares
- Occult involvement
- Out-of-control appetites
- Out-of-control tongue or emotions
- Sexual aberrations
- Suicidal tendencies
- Undiagnosable or shifting symptoms
- Violence and temper

In the Fruit step we simply note and explore these things as they come up. We trust God will bring the right things to our attention—in His timing. They cause us to be alert, to jot it down and to circle back in the Root and Boot steps to make sure these things are covered or addressed.

Sometimes we try to frame it in language we can deal with. What is really happening? For example, Bob has shared about his thought life and some ongoing torment or dark thoughts: "Bob, would you say this statement feels true: 'I experience dark, sexual and hateful thoughts that seem to want to drive me to do something vile'? How true does that sound? How would you state it to make it more accurate?" We talk back and forth until we feel we really understand it. "How does it feel? What happens when ... ?" etc.

Other times we just listen to what they say and go straight to the Root step, asking God to show us where the thing they mentioned first came up, first happened.

Root Step—Times and Doors of Entry

Recall from chapter 8 that in this step we begin probing for the source and origin of the issue. In this tool, where we are on "high DWD alert," we are specifically looking for demonic doors of entry that help explain what we saw going on during the Fruit step. We see the fruit in Bob's life and now are looking from that fruit to where or how things got started. We normally do this by asking the person if he knows, or by asking Jesus or the Holy Spirit to show us. Or we could, at this point, switch to the "Four Doors" tool and do a more thorough spring cleaning.

Demons gain influence or entry in a large number of ways, and at a specific point in time.

Demons are *opportunistic* beings—looking to gain "ground"[21] or some control over a body and mind through which they act out their particular bent or character. They choose the weakest moment and the most vulnerable place. They focus on your *metron*—your place of reflected

166

glory. Wounding and ungodly beliefs often create such opportunities.

Demons are also *legalistic* beings—they seek to take advantage of laws broken, vows or covenants made and God's commands violated to press their case of accusation and torment. Sin and entanglements create such doors.

It seems that entrance is gained by minor sin and rebellion practiced over a long period of time or a more traumatic sin or incident happening even once. It is like a cut getting infected. It takes both the cut (sin, wounding or entanglement) and the presence of the germ (demon) for infection to begin. And it takes time and acquiescence, ignorance or inattention, for it to continue and grow and expand into a stronghold. It is like a beachhead landing within us now being exploited.

Some potential entry points we and others have experienced include:

- Addictions
- Association with cursed objects and locations
- Coming under the "ministry" of demonized persons
- Curses
- Fatigue and exhaustion
- Generational or personal entanglements (vows, curses, covenants, etc.)
- Harboring unforgiveness
- Occult sin, even once
- Personal sin, blatant or persistent
- Religious spirits and doctrines of demons
- Sexual sin
- Transference at the death of a relative combined with a similar open door
- Trauma and accidents
- Ungodly soul ties in families, sexually and in abusive relationships
- Wounding, abuse, rejection

Often, and *key*, is that demons supply something that the person is deceived into thinking they need or desire. Their true will is to maintain or keep that something around even if it is killing or entrapping them.

This dynamic is often well hidden until the demonic thinks it cannot be dislodged, or is forced out, and most often is

167

initiated during childhood. For example, a traumatic incident or abusive relationship in early childhood, or simple unprotected or lonely curiosity opens the way for an agreement to be made for help and partnership with a child—perhaps appearing as a fantasy childhood friend. But it is actually a demon bent on eventual domination.

"So, Bob, where did this first begin, do you know?" or, "Close your eyes for a second. Jesus, will You show us where Bob first began to _____ or where he first learned _____?"

Bob says, "I just got a thought of a time when me and my friend next door found his father's pornography and began to look at it. I had run over there because my mom had screamed at me about something trivial. It had some women tied up or something like that. I remember it made me both scared and excited. I took it home and looked at it some more. When I was bored or angry I would pull it out. I finally just threw it away because I was afraid my mom would find it and she would blow her stack. But, I guess, from then on, whenever I felt angry at my mom I would think about those pictures. I masturbated a lot later on thinking about them."

Demons enter for one reason but they *stay* due to a continued place of wounding, unresolved entanglement, place of unbelief, perceived need or sin. In fact, the Bible says demons form "strongholds." As I stated earlier, a stronghold is a place within us that contains beliefs, attitudes and actions that stand in contradiction to God's established Kingdom order. When touched, it can feel unassailable, hopeless and unchangeable. We do not fully control it. We may feel trapped in it. That place, or those places, may or may not be inhabited but are certainly strongly influenced or controlled by the demonic, a base of operations.

In Bob's case, with more discussion we arrive at part of the root: he is trapped in self-abuse and fantasy thinking about bondage and control. But we know there is more. We feel a bit stuck and, in asking Jesus to help, we now sense

Jesus, would You help us & let us know why there is resistance? J.- tell me what is going on inside?

we are to ask Bob or Jesus to help us find a deeper reason for resistance.

Every deliverance and inner healing ministry commands demons: to cast them out, silence or bind them from interfering, etc. Some deliverance ministries listen to them as well. Some say they never listen to and get information from demons. Biblically it is not a question of right or wrong as much as preference. Jesus spoke to and listened to demons. However, in Sozo ministry, at the first responder level, we do not recommend any conversation with the dark side. Get what you need from the person and from God. Normally the person knows what is going on inside and what they are hearing. If the person is unable to keep it under control, it is time to refer to others with more experience; you did your job by recognizing the need and connecting the person with the help they need.

So, after setting the boundaries, we ask Bob to speak what he is hearing, to be the reporter:

"Bob, you are just the reporter of what seems to be happening in your mind. Just tell us what you are seeing, hearing or sensing, okay? Jesus, would You help us and let us know why there is resistance? [Pause.] Bob, what's going on inside?"

Bob: *"I keep hearing, 'I need it, it doesn't have to go.'"*

"Jesus, will You show us why the demon thinks Bob needs it?"

Bob begins to cry and speaks for himself in a flash of revelation: "My mother made me so mad. She never listened to me. I wanted to get even with her. I felt strong and powerful when I let this thing help me. It felt good to think of my mom tied up and helpless. It helped me escape, too."

We make sure that feels really true to Bob—and his tears indicate that it does. At this point we may have the (a) key. The lie is unlocked inside of Bob and he sees it clearly.

Bob had turned to bondage pictures and fantasy because they made him feel good and gave him a sense of power against a mother who made him feel emasculated and powerless.

Demonic I
you give me relief from painful reality (dreams, fantasy) in return I give you a measure of control over my mind

> *She was domineering in the home and this was Bob's way of*
> *secret rebellion against her—his way of self-empowerment*
> *even if only in his imagination. But he was trapped. He had*
> *made an unknown agreement with an unclean spirit: "You*
> *give me relief from this feeling of disempowerment and I will*
> *cede a measure of control over my body and mind." We may*
> *be ready to "Boot."*

Boot Step—Casting Out

We are now ready to take the person to "Doing Kingdom Business" and to clean out legal rights or to go to the wounding with "Presenting Jesus." We set about to undo through command what has been done by the demonic. We may go to each area and take ground back. For example:

- "I remind you that I come in the name and authority of Jesus Christ. I am His brother (sister) and a son (daughter) of the most high God."
- "I command you now to stop your evil plans, activities and schemes to steal, kill and destroy, and to submit them to Jesus at the cross. I command you to return what you have stolen from _____."
- "I demand that you release the mind of _____ in all areas in which you have gained control and influence."
- "I command that all illegal and hurtful bonds, ungodly relationship bonds and ties, the vows and curses, ungodly memberships and covenants, soul ties and all other emotional and trauma-induced bonds be surrendered, broken, dissolved and destroyed now. I command you to release your claim of right in each and every area of bondage."
- "Leave _____ now in the name of Jesus, report to Jesus and go to where Jesus sends you."

170

In Bob's case we lead him through forgiving and stopping his judgment of his mother, renouncing the covenant he made, repenting of sexual perversity, asking God to forgive him and anything else that God brings to our minds. Are we done?

We command the demon to leave. It is apparent there is an internal struggle going on. Bob yawns but feels something is "stuck in his throat." There are a number of things we could do: (1) continue to command it to submit and leave; (2) see if there are remaining rights to stay by asking the person, Jesus or the demonic (that is, go back to the Root step); (3) see if there are other demons attached to this area of sin and wounding; or (4) ask Jesus to enforce our command if we feel everything is settled.

Most of the time when we know we have dealt with lies and are ready to cast out, we simply call the demon by the name of its apparent function within the person and command it to leave, all without incident or resistance.[22] Often we lead the person to speak the commands.

The person senses a lightness, relief, inner cleanness, etc. But when we sense resistance or hindrance, when we know there is more, we then turn a more pointed focus on the reasons why.

The ability of the demonic to resist being removed is often directly proportional to the person's belief system and especially their choice, their true will and desire. If demons disobey and interfere, it is an indication (1) that they believe they have a right to stay and resist; (2) that they have something to say that is necessary to know and God is allowing it; or (3) that they are simply testing or resisting authority.

Demons will also resist if they know we expect them to resist and are not fully aware of our authority. Sometimes it is our belief system that allows resistance to occur—or more properly, our "unbelief system." You are not responsible for enforcing authority. Shouting and loud voices do not impress demons and often scare the person. It is not necessary. Those most in authority exercise it quietly, confidently and firmly. Demons shrink away when they encounter the authority of God within a believer. They "flee in terror," as it says in James 4. Bluffing on your part is as apparent as it is on theirs. Talk directly and simply. They are subordinate beings. They obey us. God seems to take a very dim view of demons that disobey a lawful command of one of His children ministering freedom. Remind them of truth about their defeat, Jesus' authority and their hot future.[23]

If we know there is nothing else to deal with in this area, then wording may go something like:

- "I command you in the name of the Lord Jesus Christ, who died for my sin and whose blood cleanses me, the true Jesus, to stand aside and stop hindering. If you refuse and choose to disobey this command, you are choosing to disobey and defy the authority of Jesus. What is your choice?"
- "I ask you, angels of God, to enforce this command now on this demon and to force compliance."
- "I command you to go and deal with Jesus because you are defying His authority."

We may ask God to show us if there is anything else we need to do or deal with. Bob begins to fidget and then blurts out that he is involved in pornography. He says, "I know that is why I am not free."

God shows him he needed to come clean, and the reality of the demonic presence shocks him into total honesty. So, in this case, we simply ask God how He wants to handle this. In Bob's case we are led to his childhood pain, use the "Presenting Jesus" tool and then return here. We now command the spirit to leave and Bob feels an instant sense of release; he gets a feeling of being clean and free. He has brought the hidden thing to the light and the cross, and the demon has nothing else to hang on to.

When all rights have been broken and ground taken, tell the demons to go where Jesus sends them. We do not teach sending demons to the pit, to hell or to dry and waterless places. We feel that is Jesus' prerogative, not ours.

In this step and subsequent ones, a few additional ways of declaring may also be helpful:

Binding and Releasing

- "I bind away from me now a spirit of _____, and choose to be bound to the Lord Jesus Christ."
- "I release this sinful habit of _____ to You, Lord, and ask You to put it to death on the cross."
- "I release any bonds I have formed with _____ and instead bind myself to the Lord Jesus Christ."

Declaring and Choosing

- "I declare my freedom from _____, from this day according to Your Word."
- "I choose today to accept, believe and receive the truth that _____."
- "I declare that God's Word says _____, and I choose today to believe God and not the lie."

Taking Authority

- "I declare my freedom from the demonic spirits of _____, from this day forth according to the Word of God, and cast you away from me."
- "I take authority over every spirit of _____, and command you to cease your activity. I cancel your assignment and order you to leave me alone and go to where the true Lord Jesus Christ tells you to go."
- "I command all demonic powers to cease their interference in this session and to be silent."

Reclaiming Lost Ground

- "I confess, Lord, that I have given away part of myself, part of my control to the kingdom of darkness."
- "I choose today to submit this part of my life to the Lordship of Jesus Christ and ask You, Lord, to reclaim and take back the ground I have lost."

Claiming Justice

- "I ask You, God, to bring the justice due me on the basis of my repentance from all known sin and on the basis of the unjust activity against me by the demonic."
- "I ask You, God, to return to me what has been stolen when _____."
- "I ask You, God, to free me from unjust influence and control when _____ happened to me."

Loot Step—Refilling

We also tell demons they are forbidden to return to their past host.[24] And we make sure that the person is filled and defended! So we now fill the Sozoee with truth instead of lies. We fill them with trust in God and surrender of those "rooms in the person's house" to the Lordship of Jesus. We ask for the Holy Spirit to fill the person. With respect to DWD we may say something like:

- "I break, cut off, destroy and dissolve any ability to re-connect with _____ and now command you to leave _____ and to go where the authentic and genuine Lord Jesus Christ tells you to go. You must report to Him now."
- "I also forbid you to return to _____. He (She) belongs to the Lord Jesus Christ, covered in His blood. If you try to return, you are willfully disobeying this command and will deal with Jesus and His angels."

With Bob we bless his choice for freedom, speak forgiveness concerning his impurity and bless him and pray that the Lord would fill the empty places in him that he filled with the false intimacy of pornography. We also prayed for the Lord to give him a true love and tenderness toward women generally and several more things.

We then give him some homework about his thought life, controls on his computer and speak with him about substitute activities and ways of replacing truth for lies. He agrees to confess all to a friend with one of us present and to partner with him concerning his walk for a period of six months.

Scoot Step—Instruction

We help a person take specific steps to get and stay clean emotionally, physically, relationally and so on. This instruction does not differ much from typical Scoot instructions except that we may help the person be alert to familiar but demonically empowered thoughts and temptations.[25]

10

The Four Doors

Search me, O God, and know my heart; try me and know my anxious thoughts; and see if there be any hurtful way in me, and lead me in the everlasting way.

Psalm 139:23–24

I think the oddest thing about the advanced people is that, while they are always talking about things as problems, they have hardly any notion of what a real problem is.

G. K. Chesterton

If stupidity got us into this mess, then why can't it get us out?

Will Rogers

What the "Four Doors" Tool Is All About

"Blood pressure . . . check. Pulse . . . check. Any aches or pains? Your blood and other lab work look okay, except your

177

cholesterol is a bit elevated, as is your weight . . . again. You *are* exercising, aren't you?"

So goes my annual physical. Checking all the signs of deterioration and of trouble is what my family doctor does best. He can burn through a standard physical in minutes and normally not miss a thing—at least not miss a normal abnormality.

The tool we call the "Four Doors" does the same thing. It is one of the major tools of Sozo and a great tool for a checkup, for a spring cleaning. It has been used as a tool for new believers, giving them a thorough screening. It works well within small groups too, with each person going through the doors with their friends. It creates a good framework and vehicle for vulnerability and the ability to tell our story, warts and all.

Some people use the "Four Doors" as a structure to organize their Sozo ministry session every time. In the hands of a skilled practitioner, it leaves the person feeling well scrubbed and clean on the inside.

It is like a spa for the soul.

Figure 8 illustrates the "Four Doors." Simply put, it is a simple combination of WESUD and the Fruit Loop applied to four key areas of sin (the four doors) that have opened a door or point of access to both demonic influence and sin's consequences in a person's life:

1. Sexual sin and soul ties
2. Anger and unforgiveness
3. Fear and control
4. Occult or false religion

This approach was pioneered during the Argentina revivals by their leaders, brought to the United States in various ways and modified and enhanced numerous times.[1] In this version of it, the rows represent sin and issue *areas*, while the columns represent sin and issue *sources*—WESUD. Using the intersection of columns and rows (one of our more colorful practitioners calls it "spiritual bingo"), you have a powerful tool to help explore a person's issues and needs and their root causes.

Let us take a more detailed look at each door.

Figure 8

Source → Sin ↓	Wounding of the spirit or soul*	Entanglements or binding actions*	Sin and rebellion*	False or ungodly beliefs*	Demonic influence*
Sexual sin and soul ties					
Anger and unforgiveness					
Fear and control					
Occult and false religion					

*Personal or generational

Door of Sexual Sin and Soul Ties

David was having trouble in his marriage. He seemed distracted by encroaching thoughts of past women. The Lord showed us a picture of his heart broken into many pieces—shattered. Each piece had been sent to someone else. He had but a fragment to give to his wife. We walked him through repenting of each instance of fornication, naming names and breaking ties. He asked for his heart back and returned the part of each woman's heart he had stolen. He repented of taking the place of the husband with "Papa's girls." When he saw that is what he had been actually doing, and understood how he had defrauded these daughters of the Most High, he wept over it for the first time. He blessed each one and declared his independence from them. We then asked God to reform his heart and make it presentable to his wife. Again he wept. We cast away demonic influences bent on keeping him trapped.

A month later he reported that his love for his wife was far fuller and stronger than ever and that he was no longer tormented by past memories. He felt clean and forgiven. He could still recall them but he now saw the memories for what they were—they had lost the allure.

Key Scriptures: Please review 1 Corinthians 6:15–20 and 1 Thessalonians 4:3–8 about two becoming one, your body as a temple of God, God's will in this, possessing your own body and the concept of defrauding another.

Basic Goal: Recognize and repent of violating God's law, another's body and your own self, and move to break harmful dependency relationships (ungodly soul ties).

Common Descriptors: perversion, lust, adultery, fornication, masturbation, rape, abuse, violence, abortion, shame, betrayal, Jezebel, unforgiveness, judgment, romantic spirit, lewdness, fantasy, hopelessness, depression, control, false romance, pornography, molestation and rape.

Ungodly Soul Ties

Because this may be a new term to you, let's discuss it briefly. An ungodly soul tie is any illicit relationship, often in which one person puts another into unclean or inappropriate control or bondage.[2] Often biblical fraud is involved, where someone promises something they cannot righteously fulfill.[3] Godly soul ties are God's provision for healthy nurturing and relationships (e.g., David and Jonathan as friends, the marriage relationship, parents and children, etc.).

The measure is *legitimacy*, not *intensity*. In legitimate relationships we learn to *bond*—to be emotionally vulnerable and physically intimate (in ways appropriate to the relationship). When the relationship is illegitimate, we do not bond; we are *bound* and we are emotionally and physically abused. Sometimes a legitimate relationship is distorted into illegitimacy (e.g., "if my children loved and honored me, they wouldn't move out of town").

Sexual sin causes soul ties. Scripture tells us that we "become one" with each such person.[4] Our hearts become shattered and divided. Memories torment and haunt us, and demonic, sexual and lust problems dog our steps toward purity. When we repent of such past fornication and adultery, bless the others, sever the ungodly soul ties, break covenants and release them to be godly wives or husbands to their present mates, we clean the slate and have the ability to reclaim a whole heart to present to our present or future mate.

Examples of ungodly soul ties include:

- family issues of dominance, dysfunction or illegitimate dependency (e.g., maternal domination or control of grown children);
- abuse of free will and domination (e.g., overcontrol of children by parents or domination by the husband or the wife, or by a person in authority), allowing a sense of control even if the person is miles away;
- unhealthy interrelationships, wherein one person controls another by their moods, threats, etc.;
- illegitimate sexual partners (both pre-marriage and during), shattering the heart and dissipating the spirit (including illicit relations between married partners);

- sexual hurt, abuse and rejection, creating a fear and control soul tie between the abuser and the victim even years after the event.

Soul ties are broken through "Doing Kingdom Business" actions, including renouncing the ungodly parts of the relationship, renouncing an unhealthy dependency on the person (even confessing idolatry), forgiving the person, taking back the part of the heart that has been given away, giving back part of the heart taken, confessing and casting out demons.

Some Specific Ideas and Approaches

We confess and repent of sin and break false or sinful relationships. These relationships can even be, for example, with the pornographic site we frequented. For this type of sin, unique as it is being against the person's own body, there needs to be a clear perspective and hatred for what is being perpetrated against the person's body and others. Often there is a need to go to the root wounding that the sexual addiction is trying to medicate. See "Presenting Jesus" for this approach. Because this sin is so common, there are many good books and ministries on this subject, and we highly recommend further reading.[5]

Typical steps or actions might include:

1. *Fruit*—Frame the issue(s) in terms of the "Four Doors" rows and understandings.
2. *Root*—Seek to know where and under what circumstances the issue got started, using the columns of the "Four Doors" matrix as a guide. Consider other tools as you go.
3. *Boot*—Take appropriate "Doing Kingdom Business" and "Dealing with Demons" actions with each issue, such as confessing sin and repenting of violating your

own body as the temple of the Holy Spirit. Break each specific soul tie or partner remembered—by name. If you cannot recall or there are many, ask God to show you one that can represent the rest. Repent of taking the place of the husband or wife in the other's life illegally.

4. *Loot*—Bless and pray for the objects of previous desire, and see them as God's daughters or sons. Give back to that person what is theirs and receive back from them what is yours; give them their heart back and take yours back, too. Sever the bonds even symbolically. Reaffirm rite of passage to manhood or womanhood and pronounce a blessing. Ask God to restore lost ground in the area of sexual purity. Fill empty places.

5. *Scoot*—Far more than most areas, the area of sexual sin relies on a strong "Scoot" component. Unlike many sins, the iniquity structure is within the body—there is also a physical-psychological mind-set, emotional and physical addiction and deep-seated lifestyle and habit patterns that must be broken. Direct practical actions that support "fleeing youthful lust,"[6] retraining and restraining the body[7] and learning how to operate the body's machinery.[8] Get rid of things, avoid situations and sever relationships that stimulate the problem. For example, destroy or disable (i.e., Internet) all connections to pornography. Commit to walking in transparency with another.

Door of Anger and Unforgiveness

Mary was a young woman I ministered to almost twenty years ago. She was brought to us by her boyfriend and was in a near catatonic state. She could not pray or even mention Jesus' name. We tried to lead her through a declaration of her intent to be free—she could not even lift her head. Listening to Papa, we began to see that she was deeply mired in pain, and unforgiveness was the lock on the door. Because she seemed to have a litany of people she held in unforgiveness, we began by asking her to write down a list of all the people who had hurt or offended her: name and offense, name and offense, name and offense.

Three pages later she had listed the four rapes she had suffered, abandonment and a long series of hurts and wounds. I explained the truth about forgiveness as described in chapter 7. Amazingly, an older woman I knew as a powerful intercessor and friend slipped silently into the room, winked and mouthed, "God sent me; go for it!" And we were off.

As her current boyfriend watched in amazement, I led her through a repeat-after-me prayer of forgiveness of each one. Name, offense, pronouncement of release of debt. She began to visibly lighten as we went through the list. We took time for her to recall, and even experience, each instance and then to choose to forgive. She picked up the pace as we entered page three and began to scream out the forgiveness like a runner on the last kick. At the end she snatched the declaration of freedom out of my hand and shouted it to the Lord and then began to sob and sob—smiling through her tears. She was so very free. And is to this day.

Key Scriptures: Please review forgiveness in chapter 7 and Matthew 5:23–24, 1 John 2:9–11 and Hebrews 12:15 about leaving your worship of God to go and make it right, how hatred causes us to stumble and roots of bitterness.

Basic Goal: Find the event or source and break it or sever it through repentance, forgiveness and releasing judgment. Address wounding as appropriate.

Common Descriptors: anger, bitterness, unforgiveness, judgment, self-hatred, eating disorders, control, betrayal, violence, murder, death, suicide, predator, failure, bitterness, condemnation, guilt, rejection, abandonment, comparison, jealousy, competition, gossip, slander, envy and desire to make someone else look bad.

Some Specific Ideas and Approaches

Forgiveness was discussed in chapter 7, and this tool takes that concept and applies it specifically. For example, hatred or unforgiveness toward a parent violates the command to honor our fathers and mothers.[9] When we break this command, no matter the condition of the parent, we set in motion a set of judgments and consequences within our own lives. When we repent of dishonor and choose to forgive and honor ("honor" is different from "obey" or to come back under control and bondage), we stop the cycle in our own lives and often free God to move in the lives of the parents.

In this tool we ask God's help to identify and list *each* person in terms of what they did—be specific and direct without making value judgments about motives or intents. Make sure the person faces honestly what has happened, even the emotion of it. Do not go forward mechanically and not from the heart, though it is a choice. You may switch to the "Presenting Jesus" tool for deeper healing of wounding.

Typical steps or actions might include:

1. *Fruit*—Frame the issue(s) in terms of the "Four Doors" rows and understandings. Look for clues to unforgiveness.
2. *Root*—Seek to know where and under what circumstances the issue got started, using WESUD as a guide. Ask God if there are any specific memories He wants to bring up. Understand each person involved and what

happened. Also look for curses or ungodly pronounce-ments spoken. Could it be generational or cultural? Consider other tools as you go.

3. *Boot*—Take appropriate "Doing Kingdom Business" and "Dealing with Demons" actions with each instance. Forgive (cancel debt owed) each person specifically for what they did. You can sometimes start with the easiest. Release any judgment you have held against them.

4. *Loot*—Speak blessing to the person you hated. Move in the opposite spirit and speak what God would want for them. Fill empty places. Pray for healing of the wounding suffered. Ask Jesus to heal or show us what He wants us to know.

5. *Scoot*—Ask God if there is anything else the person needs to do to clear their conscience. Sometimes He shows a step or action to take.

Door of Fear and Control

Betty was prim and proper. For a young woman she seemed old beyond her years. She presented very little exuberance or spontaneity. Before one word was spoken, one member of the team got a picture of her being in a straightjacket. When we approached this door she kept rephrasing the questions to avoid confronting them head-on. We finally asked her directly what she was afraid of—what thing or situation would give her the most discomfort. She struggled. We asked Jesus to give her a memory or thought—clarity. She stumbled a bit and then said, "Something that would embarrass me in front of others." She then began to cry. In the next thirty minutes she told of cruelty by her mother, who would scold and demean her in public. She seemed to shrink as she talked.

186

We began at the door of fear and control. When we felt we understood the lying paradigm in which she lived, we led her to ask Jesus if God was like that, what was true and if He could be trusted. She reported that He held her tight and whispered love to her. They walked and He held her hand in public.

We went to another open door we had noted and she forgave her mother and declared the truth. We asked if it was okay if she gave the task of "protection" to God and she cried some more as she willingly handed that exhausting job over to Jesus. We demanded the demonic leave using DWD techniques.

We blessed her and talked about ways that control was manifested, and we worked with her to recall the pictures God gave her. She drew one of them and put it in her car. She agreed to talk to a dear friend about this and to get her support. Weeks later she was greatly improved and even joined a dance club. Now that's bravery!

Key Scriptures: Please review 1 John 4:18; Hebrews 2:14–15; Romans 8:15–17; and 2 Timothy 1:7 about love casting out fear, Jesus rendering fear powerless, our adoption and the spirit we have been given in place of fear.

Basic Goal: Replace fear and associated lies with faith and trust in Papa God.

Common Descriptors: control, self-strength, predator, victimization, intimidation, fear of man, unbelief, works, performance, pride, presumption, unforgiveness, judgment, death, suicide, failure, apathy, anger, drunkenness and escape.

Some Specific Ideas and Approaches

All fear leads ultimately to fear of death, which is why Hebrews 2:14 is so powerful. If Jesus protects in the extreme, then He can protect anywhere along that path. Fear can often be linked to a misconception of the love of God—feeling it is conditional, withheld, etc. Fear most often originates in childhood relationships or events—creating ungodly beliefs. It can result in a strong need for control and reliance on self-strength. Often physical or emotional abandonment in childhood let the fear in. Movies and other media may also be a source.

Typical steps or actions might include:

1. *Fruit*—Frame the issue(s) in terms of WESUD. Look for places where there is not normal freedom to move, think, act, go, etc., as those are clues to specific areas of fear for that person.
2. *Root*—Seek to know where and under what circumstances the issue got started, using WESUD as a guide. Ask God if there are any specific memories He wants to bring up.
3. *Boot*—Take appropriate "Doing Kingdom Business" and "Dealing with Demons" actions with each instance. Renounce the fear of _____. There may be a need to forgive the one who caused the fear. You can lead the person to visualize the event and invite Jesus to help find the source and ask Him if there is anything you need to know or do—a form of the "Presenting Jesus" tool. Break any vows or covenants of protection with the demonic. Repent of things done to open a door to fear.
4. *Loot*—Declare truth about the fear; claim God's protection. Ask God to restore lost ground in specific areas. Often He will show His presence and perspective in the memory.
5. *Scoot*—Ask God if there is anything else the person needs to do to become free, even a symbolic thing. For example, when ready, the person may take an action that shows the opposite of the fear.

Door of Occult and False Religion

Tim was raised in a very strict and "quirky" church environment. As he became a teenager he rebelled and began to experiment with two of his buddies with dark music and corresponding trappings. It grew darker and darker until they were determined to find information about rituals that could influence or curse others. Then Tim met Maria and fell in love. I do not condone missionary dating, but she was a forceful young woman who simply told Tim that what he was doing was "stupid, wrong and would lead him to being more of a puppet to Satan than he ever was to his strange church."

When they came to talk, Tim quickly understood the trap he was heading for, his current state of entrapment and his alternate futures based on his current choices. This logic worked for him. He understood his need to forgive his parents and church and to renounce any ungodly bonds from both the false religious system he had experienced and the cultic practices in which he later engaged. We led him through the DKB and DWD techniques. It took some time to clean house as the Lord brought up different memories of cultic involvement. So we took our time.

Tim was elated with how he felt on the inside when we were done. We blessed him and asked God to fill him with truth and a real sense of his destiny. He immediately saw that he was destined to be a fierce shepherd and that this false direction was aimed to pervert and destroy that. When they left, he and Maria were already deep in a conversation about praying together, throwing away the music and other dark stuff and how to eventually win his two friends to God.

Key Scriptures: Please review 1 Samuel 15:23; Leviticus 20:6; 2 Corinthians 11:2–4, 13–15; and 2 Peter 2:1–3 about divination being rebellion, God's opposition to occult, deceitful spirits, God's jealousy for intimacy and the rise of false prophets and teachers.

Basic Goal: Replace demonic control with Jesus' loving Lordship.

Common Descriptors: rebellion, witchcraft, Jezebel, intimidation, control, false prophecy, lying, spiritualism, presumption, hate, spirit of the world, judgment, unforgiveness, idolatry, mocking, Ahab, false religion, mysticism and control.

Some Specific Ideas and Approaches

Much of what we see is a combination of deception and rebellion. There may be many reasons one would resort to the occult, including wounding, need for protection, healing, power or an unmet thirst for supernatural knowledge and reality. It may be entered into due to naïve curiosity and seemingly innocent practices: media, games, organizations or fantasy. It all stems from witchcraft, whether it has the patina of open and "respectable" white witchcraft or darker covert occultist practices.

Witchcraft can be defined as "demonically inspired manipulation and intimidation for the eventual purpose of control and domination." It manifests in hundreds of ways, both overt and subtle. The test is the source, not the result. At its worst the occult diverts seekers of power into demonic control. Occult includes preaching a false Jesus[10] and exercising control.[11] It includes all types of practices—horoscopes, fortune-telling, Ouija, séances (even "innocent" slumber party ones), hypnotism, palm reading, astrology, tarot cards, cultic fantasy games, etc.

Divination provides knowledge through illicit supernatural means. Sorcery is a form of this and gains control or alters the physical senses through various physical or symbolic means. There might be drug use involved. It can include binding with another or a spirit, soul ties, inner vows, etc.[12]

Some alternative medicines and medical practices are of demonic New Age origin. False religions (including false Christianity) are a type of occult practice. This can even include exaggerated denominationalism—influenced by spirits of division. Movies and music or other media can be sources of demonic influence and occult control, as can idolatry toward music and movie stars. They all have one thing in common: They are counterfeits of God's supernatural reality.

Typical steps or actions might include:

1. *Fruit*—Frame the issue(s) in terms of WESUD. Look for clues in irrational thinking, fears, control, voices, dark feelings, nightmares, violent or perverted thoughts or drives, etc.
2. *Root*—Seek to know where and under what circumstances the issue got started, using WESUD. Look for each instance or type of involvement. There is often more than one. Ask God if there are any specific memories He wants to bring up. Recognize the nature of the sin is idolatry and ultimately Satan worship. Let God stir up sorrow and realization at the reality of what has been done.
3. *Boot*—More than any other door, direct confrontation with the demonic will happen here. Take appropriate "Doing Kingdom Business" and "Dealing with Demons" actions with each instance. Confess and renounce each instance remembered specifically and break the bind with it—this is radical and takes concerted effort. Declare intention to come under the Lordship of Jesus

Christ in each area. Repent of idolatry and not trusting God, making Him jealous and rejecting His provision. Renounce each step of a ritual.

4. *Loot*—Pray for healing from the damage that resulted. Pray for filling of each area with specific truth and protection. Replace lies and the counterfeit with truth and reality. Ask for the blood of Jesus to cover and protect the person.

5. *Scoot*—Ask God if there is anything else the person needs to do to become free, even a symbolic thing. For example, they must be willing and agree to destroy all occult and cult objects, books, music, etc. There is sometimes a period of resisting Satan's attempts to reassert ownership and control. If the hold was strong, plan to walk things out with a friend as appropriate.

The "Four Doors" Walk-Through: Carol

So how does this all work together? To answer that, I have created a condensed fictitious account showing the key points in a typical session. Any similarity between this example and any specific real-life Sozo session is coincidental. Other tools may be appropriate as well, but we will limit ourselves to this tool and "Doing Kingdom Business." Notice the movement around the steps of the Fruit Loop.

The basic introductions are made and initial explanations accomplished. Everyone is comfortable and ready to go. We all spend a minute listening to God and soaking. We encourage Carol to open herself up to the Lord, and we bind any spirit that does not name Jesus Christ as Lord from interfering or hindering. We ask for angelic protection.

S: So what's going on with you?

C: Well, I've been feeling really "jumpy" for the past six months or so. Maybe a lot longer, but it's really coming to a head lately. The other day my daughter came up behind me and said something, and I screamed and almost passed out. She says I boss her around, too. And my husband says I am getting really sensitive to suggestions or even gentle criticism, where I jump down his throat whenever he suggests the smallest thing.

S: You said you are comfortable with Jesus, so let's ask Him to help you. Can you give an example? Jesus, will You show her an example to clarify things?

C: Hmmm . . . let me see. Oh, yes. The other day my husband asked me to vacuum the living room, and it's like a bomb went off inside my head and I yelled at him: "You are not my mother!"

S: Why your mother? What was she like?

C: Well, she was really wonderful in most ways, but was very strict with me—at least that's what I thought. I am kind of a dreamer with a lot going on inside my head, some say even very prophetic, and she was very practical and all business. It made me really mad, like she was always trying to control me.

We ask Jesus to bring to mind those things that are pertinent. At this point, we are getting insight into several areas to pursue. We always address what comes up, believing Jesus or the Holy Spirit will prompt the right things and memories.

S: Why do you think she was trying to control you? Jesus, what do You say?

C: Well, I don't know. [Pause.] I just got the thought that maybe she was jealous of my relationship with my grandma. I am a lot like she was before she died, and I spent a lot of time with her when I was a child. Mom said that she was into all kinds of weird things where she read fortune cards or something and told people's future. Stuff like that. So Mom made sure I went to this terrible church—so dry, boring and strict. I would sneak out when I could on Wednesday nights and go to the movies. A real rebel, huh? Then after the accident, where I was injured and Grandma was killed, I began to feel like maybe I should start doing things like that to . . . maybe sort of like to honor her memory or something.

S: The accident? Let's hold that one for later, okay?

We do not have to do a complete and complex total map of the person's needs but simply deal with what has been presented to us, leaving the rest to other times and places as God leads. At this point we are getting the clear sense that God may want us to see several open doors to explore and close, including rebellion and unforgiveness of Mom (Door of Hatred and Unforgiveness), fear from the accident (Door of Fear) and witchcraft as a result of Grandma (Door of the Occult). We'll take them in that order, though in a real session it might weave in and out a bit. There is also the probability of demonization in the areas of fear, control and the occult— maybe transferred from Grandma at the time of her death.

At this point we also have a picture of the attack against Carol's prophetic gifting and destiny call, so we overtly ask her to interact a bit with Jesus in order to awaken this call. In other cases we would simply ask Spirit-led questions, counting on the Lord to reveal and bring to mind the way we should go and the answers that should be given.

S: Let's start with your mom. Why do you think she was so strict with you? Let's ask—who are you most comfortable with: Father, Jesus or the Holy Spirit? Jesus? Okay. Let's ask Jesus if He would be willing to help you get to the bottom of things, okay?

C: Sure, that would be great!

S: Say this: "Jesus, will You show me why my mother was so controlling with me?" [Repeats, pauses.] What are you seeing, sensing or hearing, Carol?

C: Well, this is silly but I think it was because she was afraid I would end up like Grandma, into that weird stuff and all. I just remembered her saying something like I would go to hell if I did that stuff. It really scared me, and to this day I feel like I have to not pay attention to anything inside my head.

S: How does that make you feel?

C: Well, I feel really bad, I guess, because she was doing the best she could to protect me. Maybe she was afraid of her mom. She was controlling, though.

S: Are you willing to really forgive her and let it go?

C: Yes, that would be really good for her and me.

S: Then let's do a repeat-after-me prayer. I'll lead to help you with the wording—sort of like a marriage vow you want to get just right. But if you can say it better or more accurately than me, then use your own words. I am just here to help you through it. God will honor the intent of our hearts even if our words are fumbling and incomplete. Okay?

C: Sure.

S/C: [Very slowly, and with pauses to think, listen and cry.]

"Mom, I forgive you for controlling me and being very strict with me. I forgive you for making me distrust Grandma. I also forgive you for trying to force upon me a religion that does not listen to the Holy Spirit in favor of rules and controls. You did not know what you were doing and tried your best to protect me. I take back now and repent of all judgments I've held against you, as if I know better than you why you did what you did. I release you now from any inner or spoken curses from me against you, and I repent of them and of rebellious and angry thoughts against you.

"Jesus, I confess rebellion and judgment against my mom. You have said that rebellion is like the sin of witchcraft to You, and I am sorry for my participation in it. Would You forgive me of my judgments and rebellion and make me totally clean in that area according to Your promise about confession? I declare my freedom in Jesus today from any demonic control in this area, and I place myself under the blood and protection of the Lord Jesus Christ.

"I choose today to honor you, Mom, as my mother and to bless you. Jesus, will You please bless my mom and lead her into a closer and closer walk with You? Would You heal her of any fears and unforgiveness she has had toward her mom? I bless you, Mom.

"I also renounce my participation in a false religion of control and externals and ask You, Jesus, to bring Your healing and gentle presence into that place. I repent of judging them, as if I knew better, and ask You, Jesus, to forgive me for judging Your church—that is Your place, not mine. I repent of it. I submit to You, Lord, and I ask You, Lord, to take back the ground I have given away to the evil one for me. Amen."

S: How does that feel?

C: Wow, that feels real good on the inside . . . that's amazing!

S: Anything else about your mom before we go on?

At this point we might do a few other things about the mom if there were other places of rebellion or sin. We would continue to ask Jesus to show us anything there. We now turn to a different door to explore her relationship with her grandma in a way that would lead us to the times and places where she participated with Grandma in occult practices.

S: Tell me about your times with Grandma. Did she and you do some of those weird things you were telling me about together? Let's ask Jesus to show you any times or memories He wants you to see, okay? Repeat after me, "Jesus, will You please show me where I participated in things with Grandma that were false and not good for me?"

C: A couple of thoughts are coming to me. . . .

We then "Do Kingdom Business" to renounce participation, repent of it, choose the real over the false, move to "Dealing with Demons" to rebuke any demons of the occult that entered into her and ask Jesus to fill her.

S: Carol, from what you've said, Grandma had a lot of influence over you, maybe even some of it inappropriate in terms of her control and relationship.

C: Yes, that's right, she told me I was her soul mate . . . sort of funny.

S: Would you like to break that inappropriate soul tie while still blessing Grandma?

C: Yes, that would be really good—it always made me feel a little strange or inappropriate, you know, nothing sexual but just a little . . . well, violated. But I wanted her attention.

S: Let's break those soul ties—want to repeat after me? Okay. [Slow and thoughtful again . . . as always—we explain briefly what soul ties are first.]

"I repent of the inappropriate soul ties I participated in with Grandma. And I choose to sever them today, allowing only the reality of appropriate relationship to exist, even though she is now dead. I send away from me the wrong part of Grandma that she tried to put in me and to give me. I refuse it now and give it to Jesus to take to the cross. I claim my freedom from ungodly influences coming to me through my grandma. I am tied spiritually to my Lord Jesus Christ, and I ask You, Jesus, to fill that place with Your presence alone. I renounce any participation vow or covenant made with any demonic spirit through my grandmother and command you to leave my presence and go where Jesus tells you to go. I ask You, Jesus, to take back the ground I have lost in this area."

At this point a team member senses things may not be fully done and passes that information along. We ask Carol and she agrees that something is still there. We may move into part of "Dealing with Demons" and deal with identifying and casting out spirits.

Seeing the pattern of control—a subtle form of witchcraft— we lead her to recognize the control her grandma tried to exhort, her mother's control and her own attempts to control her husband and children. We "Do Kingdom Business" in renouncing, repenting, claiming freedom and choosing the control of the Holy Spirit rather than demonically inspired witchcraft.

We may also, if we sense it, go after any generational witchcraft coming from Grandma's line through forgiving past generations, repenting on their behalf, taking those things to the cross of Jesus and placing the cross between Carol and past generations, severing Carol from curses, vows and other things of the occult, asking God to allow the good things and the destiny gifts from the generations to flow fully to Carol and claiming her God-intended inheritance from Grandma and her ancestors.

Now the place is open to deal with the accident and fear. A logical next step might be to use the "Presenting Jesus" tool to go to the place of fear—but this is the "Four Doors," so . . .

S: Carol, let's talk about the accident, is that okay? Tell me about it.

C: Grandma and I were driving and a truck came out of nowhere and plowed into us. I was awake the whole time, but Grandma died. I was sort of out of it.

S: How old were you when that happened? How did it feel, and how does it feel today?

C: I think I was about five or six. It was awful, and I don't like to think about it. I avoid ever going down that street; it gives me the creeps. Since that time I still don't feel safe when I drive, like I am not protected.

At this point, based on a note passed to the leader, we might do a very short explanation about the demonic and transference, in a way that reassures her she is okay and helps her to understand voices in her head and the fear she feels—not an exposition on demonology. After she walks through the memory, she sees it and is ready.

S: Would you like to deal with the fear and the voices and bless Grandma? Let's do another repeat-after-me, okay?

C: That would be great. Let's do it.

198

S/C: "I renounce the lie that I am alone, exposed and not protected, and I choose today to rely on the truth that, Jesus, You are my protection and my shield. I renounce any other source of protection or reliance. I break any covenant I made with any demon offering protection, and I also renounce coming under the authority and influence of a demon causing fear. I renounce my participation in believing those lies of fear and I break that hold over me today and announce my covenant with the Lord Jesus Christ in the area of security and protection. Jesus, You and Papa God love and protect me, and Your perfect love casts out fear. . . . I consider it cast out today. I also declare today that Jesus Christ is my only source of spiritual information and the only One with whom I make any covenant to gain information, insight or any other form of revelation. I ask You, Jesus, to remind me of this declaration, and to teach me by Your Holy Spirit to walk in faith and trust in You, especially when I drive."

S: How are you doing? Are you okay?

C: Great, that was pretty amazing. I actually felt something lift off of me, like it was tight in my throat and then gone.

S: Jesus is Lord over all Satan's demons, and you have His authority over yourself to stay clean and clear.

After some further probing and asking if there is anything else God wants to do today, the team gets the "all clear" sign from both Carol and the Lord that the restorative work for that Sozo session is complete. So we move into blessing.

S: Carol, let's then take a little time to bless you and to thank the Lord Jesus for the places of truth and of freedom He brought you to today. How does that sound?

C: I'd like that.

We now begin to thank God and may ask Carol to verbalize her own thanksgiving. We ask for the Holy Spirit to fill her, and we return to each place of ministry asking for God to protect, fill and communicate the truth. We ask for angels to cover those places while tender and to defend her against any backlash of the demonic. We ask the Holy Spirit to help her follow through with transformation of her thinking and remind her of the key truths she heard today.

We may also speak to Carol about her prophetic destiny and show her the pattern of attack against her. We would remind her of the good coming through the generations and the demonic scheme to pervert it and turn it to witchcraft. We would help her to see that that is a sign of the power that God trusts her with and that God would like her to begin to move into that place—slowly, and under proper authority and protection within a loving church family and with older women and men who can help teach and guide her. We might have Carol specifically claim and specifically accept her calling and inheritance.

We would tell her about any follow-up activity and then bless her and send her on her way.

We then take a little time to debrief the team members and gain insight that may not have been brought forward fully. It is a teachable moment for all to gain wisdom and experience. We then turn to pray for Carol, for each other, for protection over our entire sphere and for our expectation of blessing, not backlash, in our lives. We clean up the room, turn in paperwork and . . . get a bite to eat together.

11

The Father Ladder

Two little girls, on their way home from Sunday school, were solemnly discussing the lesson. "Do you believe there is a devil?" asked one. "No," said the other promptly. "It's like Santa Claus: it's your father."

Unknown

To carry a grudge is like being stung to death by one bee.

William Walton

See how great a love the Father has bestowed on us, that we would be called children of God; and such we are.

1 John 3:1

I cannot think of any need in childhood as strong as the need for a father's protection.

Sigmund Freud

What Is Your Picture of Papa?

My friend Dawna said, "Okay, Mary, close your eyes. Now what picture comes to your mind when I say the term *Father God* or *God the Father*? Not your religious-head picture but your heart picture. What did you see, sense or feel?"

Uncharacteristically, Mary did not have a picture in her head. She felt like no one was there, a sense of absence. But she did get a vague feeling of not being okay, of angst or fear, of wanting to shrink back, of not doing quite well enough. She felt suddenly lonely. Strange—is God like that?

Could Mary see God the Father as having a celebration in her honor—especially when she did not deserve it? She did not think so. Not even in her dreams. Even though Scripture clearly shows that is His pattern.[1]

I was that way. Maybe you are, too.

I used to think that the one thing the Holy Spirit probably said inside of us after we got saved was something like, *No, stupid, not like that,* or *Maybe some other time.* You might laugh. So, smarty, what is the one thing *you* really think the Holy Spirit says inside of you? If you were deeply honest, you might say something like, *Well, you failed again,* or, *You're not quite right for the occasion,* or, *I'm pretty busy right now,* or just, *Shut up.*

That is *not* what the Holy Spirit says. This is:

> But when the fullness of the time came, God sent forth His Son . . . that we might receive the adoption as sons. Because you are sons, God has sent forth the Spirit of His Son into our hearts, crying, "Abba! Father!" Therefore you are no longer a slave, but a son; and if a son, then an heir through God.
>
> Galatians 4:4–7

Sons. Heirs. Savor that.

Scripture states that the one thing the Holy Spirit of God stresses again and again within us is, "Call Him Abba."[2] The *one* message God the Father, Creator of the universe, omnipotent, omniscient, omnipresent, wants to get across is that it is okay to call Him "Papa." He likes it.

It makes Him smile.

It conveys His heart; it opens His lap for snuggling. It allows us to see His crinkly-warm smile when He looks at us and to feel warmly accepted and loved.

No fear. No misunderstanding. No cringing. No backhand. He wants us to believe that. In fact, the real practical definition of faith is not found in Hebrews 11:1, which is faith theory, but in Hebrews 11:6:

> And without faith it is impossible to please Him, for he who comes to God must believe that He is and that He is a rewarder of those who seek Him.

If you want to please God, then believe that He is both willing and able to help you. Not willing but unable. Not able but uninterested. No, He is *both* able and willing. He wants us, above all, to know Him as one who rewards those who seek Him. He wants to be our Abba. Christianity is all about a Father who lost His kids and has set about to win them back. And once won, nothing will take them away.

The "Father Ladder" tool gets to that—and to other relationships, too: mother, siblings, Jesus, the Holy Spirit.

Basic Concept[3]

Our earliest primary relationships (father, mother, siblings) frame the reality in which we experience all relationships— especially intimate ones. When we begin to understand and try to experience intimacy with the loving members of the Trinity, that early framework, meant by God to be a boon, is often the bane in our ability to experience intimacy with God in all His aspects.

For example, the Word of God tells us what Father God is really like. That is objective truth. But our human family relationships color how we see God. As Stephen Covey said, "We see the world as *we* are, not as *it* is." We see God the Father through the veil of reality created from our relationship and experiences laid in when we were young and in the presence of our earthly father. We gain ungodly beliefs.

It is also true that we tend to see Jesus based on the treatment we received from sibling relationships, and we see the Holy Spirit colored by the nurture we received from our mother or mother figure(s). A harsh or distant mother creates within us a belief about life in which nurture is absent, tenderness is rare and hard to receive, and insecurity and a cold remoteness flavors every interaction. We come to view the Holy Spirit as these things to us . . . but it is the complete opposite of who He really is.

We may have been wounded by any or all of these, even when they are good people. As my friend Diane says, "If we think of Ward and June Cleaver as being a ten out of a possible ten in terms of parental perfection, then God is a thousand. *No* parent can fully and rightly portray God to any child." There is *always* some adjustment. And immature childhood perceptions may have warped what a well-meaning parent intended.

This tool is very good at establishing the potential for, and beginnings of, intimate relationship with Father God, the Holy Spirit and Jesus—though relatively few have a tough time seeing Jesus as a gentle, wise and compassionate friend. The goal is to reestablish relationship with that member of the Trinity.

It most often begins with our earthly fathers. I have never known someone who has a clear, intimate heart-picture of Father God who is very messed up emotionally. But problems with that relationship have created lies and false concepts about Papa God that color and block intimacy with Him. It is at the very heart of the battle—what is Papa really like? Get that one right and all else follows. When we deal with the roadblocks and clutter, then we free the person to be able to hear directly from Papa God, often through a revelatory picture.

Basic Approach

When we ask the person to picture the Father, the Son or the Holy Spirit, we can normally get a strong impression of what the relationship has been like with the corresponding family member, and what lies are believed about God. We can ask God to help the person set aside the false paradigm and reach for the true one. We can then quickly move to healing and forgiveness in that relationship using "Doing Kingdom Business" (DKB). God Himself often interacts, speaking into the person's heart in amazing ways. Sometimes the person is so afraid of the Father that we need to ask Jesus if He would be willing to assist in bringing the person to Papa God.

Figure 9 shows a basic logic sequence through the Father Ladder. It is very simple in concept. As with all the tools, we do not force anything. If we are stymied in one line, we simply go to another tool. There is *never* a sense of failure, and there are no wrong answers to any questions.

We are interacting with both the person and God throughout the process. We will walk through it with God the Father in mind here—but it works well with the Holy Spirit and Jesus, too, though 90 percent of the time a father issue is present.

We begin by asking the person to picture Papa God. We might say, "What picture comes to mind when I say *Father God*?" or, "Picture Father God and describe Him to me."

Those with a strong sense of Father's blessing and a healed relationship will always have a good, intimate picture of Father God. His face is clear and loving, they feel close and warmly loved, and have little trouble thinking of themselves in His lap, resting, not religiously doing.

Figure 9

The Father Ladder

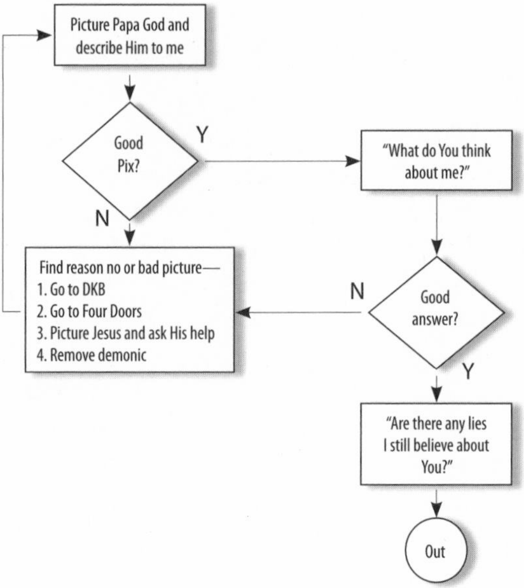

Other pictures make Papa God seem distant, stern, formal, high above and scary, seated and unapproachable, or a feeling or entity without welcoming body or form, etc. This is contrary to God's scripturally given picture of Himself to His adopted children.

When we have a "bad" picture of Papa God, we look for reasons. The reasons are based primarily on lies or misconceptions we believe about Papa God, learned through past experience with our primary father figure. These are often held in place or maintained through our understandable, but sinful, reactions to and attitudes about events, periods of time, the relationship itself or even the lack of relationship. Review chapter 2 if you are struggling here.

When we clearly understand the picture they see or feelings they experience, we might move to the Boot steps of the

206

DKB techniques, such as choosing forgiveness, renouncing lies, repenting, etc.

It might be that the person is so traumatized or so deceived concerning Papa God and the father image in general that we ask Jesus for help. We can ask the person to picture Jesus, deal with any issues there first, and then, if the person is experiencing a clear and intimate picture of Jesus, we can ask something like, "Jesus, will You take me to (or show me) Papa God?"

Often it is hearing what Father God has to say about us that brings the healing—so we can lead the person into asking, "Papa God, what do You think about me?" If there is not a good answer, we go back to find reasons using the other tools. If there is a good answer, we can go to cleaning up any related lies through asking Papa God, "Papa, are there any other lies I believe about You?" This often leads to more revelation and healing. It is a variation on the "Presenting Jesus" tool of the next chapter in that way.

We find that the picture that God gives to the person is often highly symbolic of that person's own calling. God shows us the part of Himself that we are to strongly live out and reflect to the world—that part of Him that we are. For example, a man got a picture of a fierce but kind lion. That picture prophetically showed him the reality behind his own fears and timidity, and his calling as a fierce but kind protector of the weak . . . which was his passion and the focus of the enemy's attack against him.

The "Father Ladder" Walk-Through: Bob[4]

We will use the format of a more formal ministry setting, though this could be done through simple conversation as well. The basic introductions are made and initial explanations and liability paperwork is accomplished. We sense Bob is a little tight and nervous (maybe because he pops up so often in this book!), so we take a bit more time to get comfortable.

We talk to Bob about what this kind of ministry is; it is just first aid for a wounded heart. We explain that Jesus came for this purpose and so we are spot-on in the bull's-eye of God's will for today—that this is his day. We tell him that we are not professionals, but there is nothing he can tell us that we have not heard before or probably even done before. We tell him that we could just play musical chairs and one of us could be in the "hot seat," and that we are all just brothers and that the problem is the problem, not Bob. We may chat a bit about how he heard about Sozo and got here. His job is the easiest, as he is just the reporter—telling us what he sees, hears and senses. We explain repeat-after-me prayers, making sure he will not just parrot and can rephrase all he wants, or stop anytime—especially when it comes to forgiveness.

Everyone is comfortable and ready to go. The team spends a bit of quiet time listening to God and soaking—we all settle our hearts and invite the felt presence of God into the room. We encourage Bob to open himself up to the Lord and we bind any spirits that do not name Jesus Christ as Lord from interfering or hindering but command them to release information to Bob as Jesus commands them to. We ask for angelic protection.

S: So, Bob, let's go for it. What's the thing you least want to talk about? After that it will be easy!

B: [Laughs.] Well, I have a list. In a nutshell, I am finally realizing that I am an angry person. I blow up at my wife and kids all the time. It just seems like I have this dialog going on inside my head, like I am justifying myself to myself and finding reasons for what I do.

Also I have some problems with Internet porn—nothing like every day but maybe once a month or so I just stray into something. It makes me feel ashamed and guilty, so I am not sure why I do it. . . . I'm an elder in my church and hate this "dirty little secret," you know? It makes me want to quit. I love people and helping them and watching over them seems like the greatest thing I ever do—but I seem to be so harsh sometimes. It just kills me.

My wife says I also work all the time and seem preoccupied constantly. She may be right. I catch myself staying late for no real reason.

If we sense that Bob is not used to honoring inner pictures, thoughts, senses and communication, we may take just a minute to help him to put more weight on it and show him that that is how God may want to communicate with him. We pray and ask God to bring thoughts, senses, pictures, etc., and we commit to honor them and to report them truly.

S: Bob, would you close your eyes and sort of let things happen? When I say the term *Father God* or *God the Father*, what picture immediately comes to mind; what do you see?

B: The picture that came to me was of sort of that Abraham Lincoln statue—sort of formal and distant, very good and important, sort of big and above me . . . I know God loves me and . . .

S: Bob, I'm not needing you to tell me what you think, but what you feel and sense. It's not what we think that moves us and defines us but what we really feel and believe on the inside.

Tell me about your dad. Was he like that? Distant and good, but aloof?

B: Well, he was always busy with work and gone a lot. When he was home he was always preoccupied with things: bills, sports on TV, you know. I never really felt like we spent time, just the two of us. I know he worked hard and always tried to provide for us. I remember that he forgot to take me to baseball practice and I got cut from the team because I could not get there. He never even said he was sorry, just, "I was busy."

At this point we would work with him to help him under-stand his feelings about himself and his dad, to get clarity on his places of wounding and unforgiveness, and places where he believes a lie about himself based on how he was treated by his dad. We might go to "Presenting Jesus" in a particu-lar memory, but this is the "Father Ladder," so we will limit ourselves to an approach that arrives at the lies and truth through the Father picture and revelatory questioning. Here is an abbreviated summary.

S: How did that make you feel?

B: Not very important, like I did not matter all that much. [He starts to cry, and we let him do so with a comforting hand on his shoulder.]

S: So to that little boy, how true would this sound: "I'm not as important to Dad as all those other things. I am not very valuable, and I have to prove myself somehow"?

B: That would sound very true. Seems obvious when you put it that way.

S: Would you like to forgive your dad for being distant and stern like Abraham Lincoln?

B: That would be good.

S: Then let's do a repeat-after-me prayer. I'll lead to help you with the wording—sort of like a verbal contract or vow you want to get just right. I'll do my best to reflect what you have told me. I'll try to listen to the Lord, but I make lots of mistakes for sure.

I want you to really be able to agree with what is being spoken. So if you want to say it better or more accurately than me, you can use your own words. If you feel something I say is not right, then let's stop and look at it. I am just here to help you through it. God will honor the intent of our hearts even if our words aren't perfect. Okay?

B: That sounds fine to me.

At this point we anticipate that as we launch into this place of speaking forgiveness that the Holy Spirit will lead us, maybe with Bob unaware, into a prophetic direction of saying and sensing things that are key to Bob's places of hurt. We might, for example, get a picture of a little boy and sense his feelings and speak from there, go to a memory and speak forgiveness from within that place, speak things as they really are without sugarcoating or making excuses so the forgiveness can be from the darkest corner of wounding and pain, etc. Bob repeats, changing some of the words and crying throughout.

S/B: Okay, repeat after me: "I forgive you, Dad, for not loving me enough to spend time with me; for not showing me that I was significant and important to you. I forgive you, Dad, for being preoccupied with other things when we were together and for making me feel like I had to compete for your love. I forgive you for seeming to be aloof and stern and important but not intimate, kind, gentle and humble with me when I was a little boy alone in my room and wanting my dad to come find me. I forgive you for not taking me to ball practice and making me get cut from the team because you felt you had more important things to do. I forgive you for always making me feel that the things that were important to me were stupid and small and for teaching me the lie that God is that way, too. I choose today to stop judging you for your actions as if I knew why you acted the way you did but to leave all judgment to God. I choose instead to bless you and to ask Papa God to bless you and to fill you with the knowledge of His grace and love. I honor you as my dad today and for the rest of my life."

We ask the Holy Spirit or Jesus to show us if there is anything else that would keep Bob separated from Father God. We may handle a few things with "Doing Kingdom Business," or go off on a longer side trip. We may encounter and use the information in "Dealing with Demons."
Then:

S: Let's picture Father God again, and this time let's ask Him to give you His own picture. [Pause.] What are you seeing or sensing now when you picture Him?

B: Well, He has invited me to come up but I still feel like I cannot go there. It just seems scary or inappropriate or something—like I am barging in on something important, like caring for China or something.

S: Let's try this. When I ask you to picture Jesus, what comes to mind?

B: Oh, He is great, like He is so loving, you know, and died for me and . . .

S: I know all those wonderful things, but let's see if Jesus would give you a picture of Himself just now. [Binding religious spirits under our breath.] Repeat after me: "Jesus, would You show me a picture of Yourself now?"

B: I just keep hearing, "I'm not worthy to see Jesus." Like it's my old Sunday school teacher saying I need to try harder or Jesus will not want me to be His friend. It's like there is this block there and Jesus is on the other side of it, but I cannot connect with Him for some reason. It feels kind of like I am trapped or stuck.

Sensing it is demonic in nature, perhaps a religious spirit, we ask Bob what he feels he is hearing on the inside—does he feel accused?

B: I keep feeling like I'm a pervert and going to hell because of the pornography.

S: Okay, Bob, let's go after the pornography thing. What do you feel inside when you decide to view Internet porn?

B: I feel lonely and empty, sort of alone, bored, too.

We may chat a bit about that and then . . .

S: Repeat after me: "I renounce the lie that I am insignificant to God and that He is cold and distant and has little time for me other than to bark orders or corrections. I renounce the lie that when I feel alone, pornography is what I need to feel better. Today I choose You, God, and not another medication. I repent of choosing pornography instead of You. I call it idolatry and I break any covenant I have made with any provider, model or other participant in pornography. I sever it now. I declare myself covered and made clean by the blood of Jesus Christ, and I take this sin to the cross and leave it there. I am sorry, God, for this and ask Your forgiveness, and I thank You for Jesus' death for my sin—I claim it now."

We might probe for any other areas and may recall the demonic and demand to know if they have any other ground to interfere. After that is settled we may command them to leave and go where Jesus sends them or we may wait till the end. If we know more than one is there, we would command them all to be bound together and be cast out all at once.

S: I now command you unclean and religious spirits to leave Bob and to go where Jesus tells you to go.

B: It's like something is sliding up my throat. [Coughs.]

S: You must go *now* in the name of the Lord Jesus Christ.

B: [Coughs again.] What was that?

S: Well, it looks like you had company; somebody does not want you to get intimate with Papa and Jesus, that's for sure. Let's disappoint him, what do you say? Want to ask to see Jesus again?

B: Sure . . . oh, that was easy; we're walking in some grass, like a park with buildings all around. Oh, yes, it's like in Washington, D.C.—weird. I can see where Lincoln, well, where Father God is sitting far ahead.

S: Would you like to do a brave thing? [Nods.]

S: Say this: "Jesus, would You take me to see Papa God?" [Pause.] What's happening now?

B: [Laughs.] Jesus is saying, "I'll race ya," just like my brother used to do.

S: Would you like to? [Nods.] Well, ready, set, go!

B: [Laughs.] I beat Him! I think He let me—we're right in front of God, down below.

S: Would you like to go closer to Him? [Nods.] Ask Jesus to take you to Him. Ask, "Jesus, would You be willing to take me to see Papa God?"

B: Yes, really. Oh, that's cool! I'm sitting on His lap; He has His arms around me and is crying. [Cries.]

We wait for a while, not wanting to interrupt something God seems to be initiating on the inside of Bob. Is this just mental? Bob would tell you it is more real than anything he has encountered religiously for a long time. Bob seems to be ready and we get a nudge to do one more thing, to go after one key lie Bob still lives with.

S: Are you still feeling brave? [Nods.] Then ask this: "Papa, what do You think of me?" [Long pause.]

B: Wow . . . He says He has been just waiting for me to finish what I was doing and that He has all the time in the world for me. I'm His favorite. [Cries.]

S: How does that feel to you? Does it sound good and true?

B: It feels really good—I feel like it is true, you know. I really do. Wow! He just handed me a shepherd's staff and said, "Welcome to the team." [Cries.] That's so awesome, I feel . . . man . . .

We may just soak for a while and thank Papa. We would then begin to speak over him about his destiny as a shepherd and as a gentle person who may be intense but is neither angry nor impure. We would reaffirm Papa's love for him and help him to hold on to what he hears Papa say to him. We might relate a bit about how much God likes to speak to us and that the things He says are ours to keep—no matter who might try to steal them away from us—they can be life changing. We help him to Scoot the porn out of his life through wise choices and controls.

12

Presenting Jesus

Everyone stumbles over the truth from time to time, but most people pick themselves up and hurry off as though nothing ever happened.

Sir Winston Churchill

The LORD is near to the brokenhearted and saves those who are crushed in spirit. He heals the brokenhearted and binds up their wounds.

Psalms 34:18; 147:3

Logic will get you from A to B. Imagination will take you everywhere; it is more important than knowledge.

Albert Einstein

Jesus Speaks

It was 1992. Toni was not a believer—well, not in my then-narrow interpretation anyway. So you can imagine her surprise when I asked her what she thought Jesus might have to say about her being taken out of her abusive family and placed in foster care—how Jesus felt when five-year-old Toni was being forced from her mother. Toni said, "I don't know—how would I know that?" "Well, for me, it is kind of simple," I replied. "I just close my eyes and look for Him and just try to ask Him and see what He says to me on the inside and . . . "

I was about to launch into some conversation designed to tell Toni that she needed Jesus in her life. It was my turn to be surprised when Toni, with eyes shut, interrupted, "He says He was sad, too, but would never leave me alone."

"He what!?"

"I guess that's Jesus, huh? Like you said, He sounds so close and friendly."

"Ah . . . well . . . yes, sure . . . "

I guess He *is* near to the brokenhearted.

Back then I was surprised when Jesus answered directly. Today I am surprised when He seems not to.

Overview of the "Presenting Jesus" Tool

One of my favorite movie scenes is in *The Matrix* when they are about to put Neo into the matrix for the first time. Morpheus, the old father figure, says, "This may seem a little strange at first." And then, wham!—he suddenly appears in a different world. One with cooler clothes.

Neo has to learn that his perceptions are not totally aligned with reality, and that his own belief can change the dynamics of that world. He learns that his beliefs are the limiting factor. To prove it Morpheus leaps two hundred feet to another rooftop.

This tool is just a little bit like that. Like all of Sozo, this tool is based directly on the truth that God Himself wants to interact with us and bring healing.

This tool is derived from a set of related methods that was originated by various practitioners, and it is influenced by the "inner healing" of the 1970s, and by the ancient art of "listening prayer" currently experiencing a revival of interest.[1] We had been encountering and interacting with Jesus for a while in ministry settings when we saw (much to our relief) that many others were also growing in this understanding of ministering through an interactive session with God Himself (thus our Partners with God foundation).[2]

For example, Dr. Ed Smith of Theophostic Ministry has developed an effective use of this basic truth and is a most prolific writer and demonstrator of this method.[3] As in all the tools and techniques, our approach takes the best of these streams and is mixed with our DNA and foundations.[4]

If you have forgotten (or skipped—surely not!) the content of chapter 5 about honoring the flow of God, His voice, His ways, His willingness to enter into our pain and need with truth and grace, I recommend you do a quick review there and then read on here.

When you ask God a direct question, like any good father, mother or friend, He will respond—mostly in familiar and safe ways, but often in surprising ways, too. This may stretch our paradigm about God somewhat—and maybe that is a good thing. In this tool we keep within the safe boundaries of simply asking God and listening.

For example, I was with Vinnie when we asked Jesus if He would be willing to help him tear down the strongholds of fear in his life. I expected a simple "yes." But, and I can see God's fun-loving smile here, Vinnie suddenly saw himself in a jet cockpit bombing forbidding stone castles. He even began leaning left and right in his chair. One castle would not fall. We asked Jesus why. Jesus said, "Let Me fly." So he changed places with his "co-pilot," who did things he could never do with that jet. He even felt a bit airsick as the last stronghold of fear was blasted to smithereens. Only later did he tell me both his father and grandfather had been fighter pilots, and that he had felt he had failed by not following in their footsteps. To this day he recalls what happened as a gift from God just for him and smiles. So cool!

It would be hard to put that in a set of easy-to-follow steps, huh?

This tool's strength and primary target is addressing inner wounds ("captive" versus "prisoner") and the internal structures that keep us from healing. This tool focuses on the understanding that we are best healed from past wounding by hearing God tell us what is true and what He thinks.

How is this so?

Recall the discussion in chapter 4 about the growth of a stronghold. A wounding occurred in the past, normally in childhood. Our wonderful minds, often with demonic assistance, constructed a false reality to account for and deal with the wounding. We then live within that construct and build upon it. It seems true to us—so it plays out that way in our world. It's what we believe about what happened that is important, our perception of reality at that time.

We may, in response, have exhibited sinful reactions of anger, fear, hatred and unforgiveness, and developed sinful ways to escape or mask the pain. But these are secondary issues—important, but not central.

When something happens in the present that feels somewhat like the old pain, it is like hitting a bruise—there is an overreaction. We (or worse, our spouse or friends) walk into an emotional minefield. That inner lie structure amplifies past pain in present circumstances. Present emotions and issues reflect the past event.

Using this current-day "Fruit," I can follow it back to the point of origin. God (normally Jesus, but we sometimes ask which member of the Trinity the person is most comfortable dealing with) accelerates the process amazingly by bringing the person right to the point in time when the lie was first believed, the pain first incurred, the confusion implanted. Sometimes it is a memory that is typical, representative or even symbolic of what happened repeatedly but is somehow the "right" memory.

When we allow the Lord to be with us, remove the lie and replace it with truth, the pain can drain out.

So we ask Jesus to communicate what is true about that situation, maybe where He was, maybe what He thinks about it. The person does the questioning through our repeat-after-me leading and facilitating. This often leads to other restorative exchanges with Jesus and Papa God in terms of loving revelation, healing, memories explained, destiny assured and fears calmed.

How to Use the Tool

Figure 10 shows a basic "logic flow chart" through "Presenting Jesus." The steps in the diagram are typical but not rigid. It is very simple in concept. We do not force it. If we are stymied in one line, we simply go to another or to another tool. There is never a sense of failure, and there are no right or wrong answers to any questions asked . . . ever. And we are not trying to dredge up every bad memory—only the key place God would like us to go to correct a false belief on which part of the person's life is based.

Define Feelings of Pain and Wounding

Our goal for this step is to end with the person saying, "I feel *this* negative emotion often, it leads to *this* harmful dynamic in my life, and it seems to point to *this* lie I strongly believe." That would be perfection—but even close works well.

We listen for words and phrases that are keys to strongly held beliefs ("I feel lazy," "I can't ever . . ." etc.). Ask who, what, when and why questions to clarify for the person. Ask, "How did it feel when . . . ?" The lies can be about themselves, others, the world or God.

Figure 10

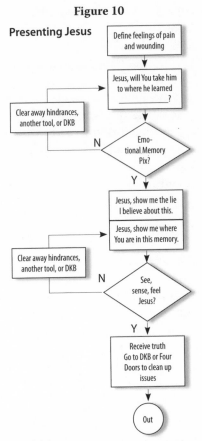

Presenting Jesus

Maybe there is a recent event in which they overreacted. What did they feel when this happened? Was there an accusing inner voice saying anything to them? What did they think about themselves or the circumstances when that happened—"I felt that . . ."?

Look for deeper emotions behind presenting ones. For example, sexual lust masking loneliness, anger masking rejection. The deepest emotions are often experienced early in life, long before they could be given names.

Never direct, control, manipulate, explain, make assumptions, judge, imply or force your opinion on anyone.

Ask clarifying, not leading, questions. Do not put words in someone's mouth, ideas in their head. Do not even go near suggesting memories by mentioning that a specific person might have harmed them, done something to them, etc.

If you can, seek to frame what they are feeling and echo it back to them. You might ask something like, "When you are feeling that way, how true does this phrase sound: _____?" To sharpen it you might ask, "How would you state it to sound more true to your heart, not your head?" Try to keep them from logic or explanations.

If it seems simple and clear, you can sometimes even just ask Jesus what is true and to bring healing without all the memory work in the next Root step, but this is rare. In those cases we simply ask, "Jesus, what do You say about this . . . ?" or, "Jesus, would You tell _____ what is true?"

Find the Origin of the Pain

Our goal for this step is for them to be able to experience an event that leads them to say, "I *first* believed that lie right here. That is where the pain began." Or, "This event seems very significant in understanding where my problems came from and how to dismantle them."

We look for first occurrences or origins of the memory. Often we help the person float loosely back in time until they seem to "land" on a memory or thought that is earlier than the one they first present. You may simply ask Jesus to take them to the place where they "first learned the lie that ____."

Often when we ask God for help, the very first thing that comes up is key—even if it feels silly. A standing joke in this ministry is hearing someone say, "Well, I just had this silly thought," "I haven't thought about that for a long time" or "I forgot all about this until you asked. . . ."

We rarely settle for memories that are past the age of twelve for deeper character-forming wounds. However, wounds that involve affirmation, destiny and the blessing of manhood or womanhood often happen at puberty.

This is not court testimony or counseling. We are not looking for explanations or a place to put blame, but to understand their perceptions. Memory is a tricky thing. First of all, it is the person's *perception* of the event we are dealing with. No one recalls everything from a true perspective except God. What "feels" true and what "is" true are different. Second, emotional and traumatic memory is often detailed and exact and stored in a bottled-up and high-pressure state. It may explode. Simple recall is not like that; it mostly consists of the brain reconstructing a reasonable facsimile of the event from a few stored facts.[5]

Memories are sometimes clarified or enhanced when we stir up visual or emotional parts of the brain. We are careful not to ask the person to go deeper than we feel God is leading, but we do not shy away from letting the person experience strong emotions. We can ask them to describe the room, an object, etc. We may allow the person to pour out their feelings about the situation—sometimes talking directly to Jesus. We always ask gently.

Sometimes, to make the person more comfortable, we ask Jesus if He would be willing to meet them in a safe place prior to going to the memory. Sometimes we address the naïve childlike spirit of the person first with words of comfort and encouragement and blessing. We then ask the spirit part's help in bringing the person to a conscious memory.[6] It is almost like asking a child, "Where does it hurt?" and watching them point to a sore spot on their body.

We believe in and properly use prophetic gifting. Remember our foundation about being partners with God. We dishonor God both when we "despise" and avoid the prophetic *and* when we grieve God by its wrong use. Your prophetic insights are to be used to ask wise questions, to help nudge toward a memory or thought and to help overcome hindrances, *not* to take the place of Jesus in ministry.

It is normally best when we simply use those revelations to help us as facilitators of an encounter with God. If it *is* God, it will bear fruit and be evident without our saying so. But we are not shy about asking about an inner impression we received—but we ask gently with a totally open hand.

If someone has trouble seeing, we encourage them with the truth that Jesus is an ever-present help in time of need and will never leave them or forsake them. We may also need to deal with lies or the demonic that are blocking the expectation of the person that God would want to speak to him, or that he needs to stop the process right now, etc.

Be aware of false, demonic, red-eyed "Jesus" figures masquerading and speaking harshly, falsely religious, etc. Take authority and demand it identify itself or be gone. Use DWD. At God's leading you can remove hindrances through renouncing, confessing, stilling voices, forgiving, etc. They tend to be lies, sin issues or demonic. Let Jesus show you if there is a block to freedom. He will.

Hear Truth, Bless, Fill, Proclaim

When present in the memory, we ask Jesus to bring truth, to tell what He thinks, to show where He was or what He was doing. We ask the person to be a reporter—what they are seeing, sensing or hearing about Jesus and His presence—allowing Him to do what He wants to do, to bring truth in any way He chooses.

It is very effective to carry on a three-way conversation with Jesus, asking Him things like, "Jesus, will You bring truth about this situation?" "Jesus, what do You feel about this?" "Jesus, what do You have to say about this?" or, "Jesus, what is true?"

It is an amazing and deceptively simple dynamic. For example, the person is feeling small and vulnerable and has believed a lie that Jesus cannot be trusted. We could quote a ton of Scripture saying He can. But that addresses adult logic, not childlike fear. So we can simply refer the fear to Jesus and ask the person, while in the memory, to ask Him, "Jesus, is it true that You can be trusted?" When He says "yes," it seems trite to us as adult observers. But it is very impacting to the little one in the memory. I have often seen someone visibly relax, open up and be freed on the basis of that simple exchange.

Jesus is timelessly present with them in the painful memory. I am not. His way works best. I have to be secure enough to trust Him. We are not changing memories or telling Jesus what to do. Jesus can communicate with pictures, words, symbolic acts, simple presence, gestures or facial expressions, etc.

For example, in one case the girl heard nothing but instead saw Jesus lying beside her, taking the worst of the pain so she could bear it. In another instance, a young man saw Jesus holding his heart in the midst of a difficult accusation—protecting it. In another situation, Jesus took a girl away with Him when a rape happened.

Complete the session with blessing and asking, "How does that feel?" Pray for them and establish the truth—repeat it to them, or ask them what they know to be true. Speak blessing and express joy at what Jesus has done. Be aware of a counterattack of doubt. Use DKB as appropriate to renounce lies or entanglements, to forgive and so on. Send demonic influence away.

Remember the Scoot step and see what God may direct you to say to help them walk things out. Sometimes so much is hung on their lies that they have a hard time figuring out who they are after the session. Help them find comfort in letting the same Jesus they met in the memory help them every day.

Presenting the Jesus Walk-Through: Ted[7]

The basic introductions are made and initial explanations accomplished. Everyone is comfortable and ready to go. The

Sozo team spends a bit of quiet time listening to God and soaking. We encourage Ted to open himself up to the Lord, and we bind any spirits that do not name Jesus Christ as Lord from interfering or hindering. We ask for angelic protection. See other tool examples and the typical Sozo section for more on the introductions.

One or more of the team members have gotten pictures or words that they write at the top of their notepad and hold to see what God may want to do with them—knowing that they might be totally or partially wrong. During the beginning of the session, a team member passes a note to the leader. It says, "Grade school, maybe third grade, I see him standing with a uniform on." We hold on to it and just see.

S: So, Ted, what's going on with you? What brought you here today?

T: Well, I'm not getting along with my wife in the area of religious stuff. She keeps trying to get me to do things, and we argue a lot. She just seems to be nagging all the time about me being more spiritual, and I would like to find a way to get her off my back.

S: Hmmm . . . well, we cannot really help her, you know— you are the intended victim today! [Smile.]

T: I'm here just to find out if the way I am is okay, I guess. I'm not very religious, you know—I kind of leave that to my wife. Every time I try to read the Bible or pray, it just seems dull, and I can't really think of anything to say.

S: Well, let's ask God to show us where to start—I bet you're a lot better at it than you think. . . .

We proceed to tell him briefly about getting pictures or words or sensing things inside and ask him to be the reporter; he reluctantly agrees. We chat for a bit and then, when we feel we are zeroing in on a key lie, we ask . . .

S: Ted, how true does this sound: "God will never be real to me because I am not very spiritual"?

T: Well, that sounds sort of true, on a scale of 1 to 10 maybe a 6 or so.

S: What would sound more true to you—more toward a 10? Jesus, would You be willing to help Ted here?

T: Well, I didn't say this back when we first started, but I just felt it again. I felt a twinge of fear—like feeling ashamed.

S: So how true does this sound to you: "Being spiritual is painful and shaming"?

T: I would say that feels very true—maybe a 9 or 10.

S: Let's ask Jesus if He would be willing to show you a memory that has meaning to you. Ted, close your eyes and let yourself begin to drift back. Jesus, will You help Ted to think of a time when he first began to believe the statement that "being spiritual is painful and shaming"? [Pause.] Are you getting anything?

T: Not really.

S: Ted, one of the team members kept hearing "third grade." It may not mean anything at all. Does third grade mean anything in this context?

T: No . . . well. It is kind of silly, but my private Christian school was kind of strict, with uniforms and all. I don't think it was the third grade, but I do remember a time—wow, haven't thought about this for years [we all smile]—I was asked to stand up and pray one day. When I stood up and tried to pray, I started stuttering and shaking and just froze. It was awful. I was so embarrassed and scared and ashamed. My teacher said, "Ted, sit down" in a kind of mean way, and everyone laughed. Then she called on this other guy. I hated him, and he said this great prayer. I just sat there and thought, *I'm never doing that again.* Kind of silly, huh?

S: Maybe not to a little boy trying to fit in. Besides, it seems God brought this one up, so let's go there, okay? Close your eyes and go to that memory if you can. How did it feel to you? Describe the classroom. Tell me how you felt.

226

At this point we are stirring up the memory to make it very vivid. We are attempting to uncork the bottled-up emotions tied to the memory. Ted describes the room and is clearly warming up. He describes the kids' faces, the mean teacher, his own shaking hands and feelings of being exposed and alone.

T: I was so ashamed; I just wanted to crawl into a hole. I felt all alone and like a total failure—it was so painful. [Tears up.]

S: You felt alone. To that little one, how true does this sound: "I'm a shameful failure when I try to be spiritual"?

T: Yes, that's about it. Maybe not all of it, though.

S: "And I'll be rejected and cast aside for someone better."

T: Yes. That's a 12 out of 10, for sure. [Tears up again.]

S: Let's ask Jesus where He was when that happened. Look around the room. Ask this: "Jesus, will You show me where You were when that happened?"

T: He is standing behind me with His hands on my shoulders, holding me steady. [Cries.]

S: Ask Him this: "Jesus, what do You think about what happened? What is true?"

T: [Pause.] He says I'm an evangelist.

The team looks up in surprise—that is not at all what we asked or expected. That is our God.

S: How does that sound to you?

T: I've always known that.

S: Really?

T: Yes, I just never wanted to think about it.

S: Let's ask Jesus if there is anything else He wants to say to you or show you. "Jesus, is there anything else?"

T: I need to forgive the teacher.

S: I want you to really be able to agree with what is being spoken. So if you want to say it better or different than me, feel free to use your own words. If you feel something I say is not right, then let's stop and look at it. I am just here to help you through it. God will honor the intent of our hearts even if our words aren't perfect. Okay?

We "Do Kingdom Business" and lead him through forgiveness. Then, with sudden insight we explain a little bit, ask permission and lead him into renouncing the lie he believed about his destiny, repenting of his fear to step into being an evangelist and breaking the agreement he made to stay away from spiritual stuff in exchange for protection from shame. We command all spirits involved in this to leave.

Over the next few weeks his wife notices that he is really taking a leadership role, even if somewhat awkwardly. Ted has to figure out who he is after the Sozo, as he has built so much of his life on the lie of being unspiritual and needing to protect himself. To realize that the opposite is true is a real shock. As much as a year later, a couple of follow-up sessions clean up ancillary things, and Ted begins to move with real authority into his destiny calling. His wife sees that she had read Ted right but did not have the tools to gently help him into it. Her own Sozo dealt with control issues and deep wounding from her mother. Today Ted and his wife are strong ministers together and have begun a church targeted at nonreligious "misfits."

Epilogue

Well, that's it. There is so much more I want to share with you. But I am confident that this framework will launch you on your way. And I am more confident that as you launch, you will find God to be a help in time of need.

But I do want to end with the story I began with in chapter 2. Remember Betsy? In closing, let's talk about our time with her. It illustrates the tools well.

We were sitting in our living room, just a normal night of reading and coffee. Then . . .

Betsy knocks at our door, comes in, sits down and asks if she can talk. Tears well up in her eyes. "I'm sorry I'm falling apart. I needed someone to talk to. I hate to take up your evening. Is that okay?"

"Sure, sweetie bear, you are worth a thousand nights!" She cries. My wife holds her. We wait. We sense Papa God gently enter the room. It is time.

My wife glances at me—"Go for it," her eyes say, "let's change the world right now." Click. On goes the tool belt.

Betsy was at a party and said something she thought was dumb. She suddenly had to flee and found herself alone in a separate room feeling stupid and sad. She didn't know what to do, so she drove around in her car until she found herself at our driveway.

I ask some questions, gently probing, seeking to go from Fruit to Root. "Tell me how it felt when you were sitting alone in the room."

"Stupid, like I was just so stupid and always messing things up."

"Have you always felt like that? Does it feel real to you, that you are a 'mess up'? Would you be willing to let Jesus help you explore that feeling with us?"

"I don't know. Sure . . . I guess."

Snap, grab the "Presenting Jesus" tool.

Several other questions about family, growing up, siblings. Being the oldest. Close your eyes and drift back.

"Your job is easy. You are just the reporter of what is happening inside you. That is where the pain is and that is where God wants to go. Okay?" A nod and a hopeful weak smile. That's all we need. God doesn't need *great* faith, just simple willingness.

"Let's ask Jesus if He would be willing to help you remember a time when you felt like a stupid failure and like you messed things up. Let Him take you to a memory, if He wants to, that sort of defines a place you began to think that way about yourself. This may seem sort of strange, but let's just try it. Okay? Ask Him something like: 'Jesus, will You show me when I first began to feel stupid and like I always messed things up?'"

"Ummm. Sure. [Pause.] Oh, wow. I know. That was easy. It was the night my mom died. My dad told me to watch her while he got some sleep. And, and . . . I fell asleep and she died. I woke up and there she was sitting in a chair and I felt like it was all my fault. I felt so alone and stupid. I messed up so much!"

A tear trickles down her cheek. She hides her face with her hair and folds her arms across her chest. Slowly the memory flows and she begins to sob and shake. My wife

230

moves to place a hand on her shoulder, letting the emotion spill out.

"I know you feel alone right now. Let's ask Jesus where He was when that happened. What He thought about all that. Can you see yourself in the room?"

Nods.

"Ask Him, sweetie."

"Jesus . . . Jesus . . . will You show me where You were when my mom died and I felt stupid?"

Long pause.

She is clearly looking at her inner screen of memory. It has come alive. I realize immediately she is quite gifted in seeing—some hear, some see, some sense, some just seem to stumble into truth and we are not sure how. It is all fine. Some get nothing and that is fine, too. It may mean there is a barrier of sin that needs to be handled first. It may just mean we should go another direction not so subjective at first. God can talk in a way that anyone willing can hear Him, that is for sure.

"Honey, what's going on inside?"

"This is funny but I see Him standing with His arm around me. I can both see it like a picture and feel it like His arm is really there right now."

"How does it feel?"

"Good."

"Ask Him if it's true that you are stupid and messed things up with your mom."

Long pause. We let things take time. We give inner things a voice. We sense when it is vivid and alive and also when the person begins to switch to analysis mode.

"Honey, what are you seeing, sensing or hearing?"

"He says it's not my fault at all. I was only eight." More sobs. "My mom is okay and happy with Him right now—that's so good!"

"Does that feel true to you?" More long sobs and shaking. "How true does that sound to that little eight-year-old Betsy?"

"True . . . wow . . . it feels true. I never thought that I was too little to do anything anyway. Why did I think that?"

It is not time right now to tell about the devil's inopportune attacks and his unfair accusing whispers that shackle us to seeming truth—all lies from the father of lies.[1] *It is enough to let her experience healing waters, oil or whatever she seems to be feeling.*

"How do you feel, sweetie?"

"Really warm and good. I just want to sit for a moment."

We sit and enjoy. Like a good massage on the inside, Jesus' healing begins. It is rippling through her psyche. We wait awhile. Basking. Let's do some Kingdom business.

"Want to forgive your dad for the way he handled it when your mom died? He needs it, I think; do you? And your stepmom, too; she loves you so."

We walk through forgiveness. More tears. Obeying God's Word to choose forgiveness.[2]

"Let's deal with the lies you told yourself. Let's begin to tell yourself the truth. Want to repent and renounce and put the lies away forever?"

A little help in what to say and do. Breaking bad contracts. Making good ones. Death and life is in the tongue. Giving account for our words.

"I keep hearing something angry, almost cursing and screaming. It makes me scared. Is that just me?"

"Do *you* think it's just you?"

"No."

It seems it is time to send enemies away with the "Dealing with Demons" tool. Resist the devil and he will flee from you.[3]

"Let's send away the voices in your head, too, and undo any bad deals you made when you were little, okay?"

"I'm not sure how."

"That's okay. We can help you. We'll lead you through a declaration and prayer. But if we say something you do not understand or wholeheartedly agree with, stop us and let's talk, or just say it in your own words. We want it to be yours, not just repeating like a parrot. Okay?"

We lead her through a repeat-after-me prayer and declaration, helping her say the things she wants to say but is unsure how to express. We identify the strategy and lies. We tell whatever spirit that has been trying to control her to stop, we invoke the name (authority) of Jesus and issue a command. There seems to be some resistance. We are stumped. We feel a need to ask another question.

"Jesus, will You give us the truth we need here?" [Pause.]

"Are you hearing or sensing anything, sweetheart?"

"I keep hearing inside my head that no one will protect her. She needs me. I feel sort of unsafe and vulnerable. I think I'm scared."

We realize the liar is being forced into the open to talk. Some part of her is afraid to be left alone. Not being able to trust a God who would take her mother, she had turned to another voice offering false comfort. She was in the classic "double bind," where she desperately needed protection and comfort but was fearful of God—damned if she did, and damned if she didn't. It is an ungodly belief. There are several directions we could go. We take the most direct.

"Sweetie bear, when this happened to you, it seems that you found a way to cope with your pain and fear and rejection. Now that you are older, it seems from what you have said that that way is not working out so well. Would you be willing to trust Jesus with that job?"[4]

"I'm not sure. Would Jesus really do that?"

"Let's ask Jesus if He would take that hard job of protecting you. Go ahead and ask Him."

"Jesus, would You be willing to protect me from evil? [Pause.] He smiled and laughed and put His arm around me like when I was little in that room. Like He is saying, 'You already know the answer, Betsy.'"

"Okay, just go ahead and give Him that job then—just hand it to Him."

"Okay, I have given it to Him."

"Where is that little girl? How does she feel?"

"Very safe. Like I am in this secure place with Jesus, held by Him. Wow, so safe! Jesus *will* protect me, won't He?"

"He said so.[5] Ready to tell that dark voice to leave you?"

"So ready!"

"Let's say this: 'I break every deal for protection I ever made with any false comfort and any spirit promising protection. I declare that Jesus, who died for me, is my protection and I need no other. Go *now* to where Jesus sends you.'" [Pause.]

"How are you doing; what's happening inside?"

"I feel peaceful. Wow, really peaceful. Nothing is there but me and Jesus!"

Let us try something else. Snap, click. She is still afraid of Father God. Let's see. Do I have permission? Yes, I think so. On to the "Father Ladder" tool.

"Want to do something else? Okay, what does God look like to you . . . Father God, I mean? What is your heart picture, not your religious head picture?"

"Well, I know this isn't right, but you asked how I feel, right? I feel like He's kind of busy and like He is looking for me to mess up."

We share just a little about His love for her, being careful not to manipulate but just to give simple objective biblical truth. One minute. It is sort of like telling a good friend about some wonderful things another friend said about them. Papa thinks about her a million times a day, and even numbers her hair.[6] He has an eternal home for her and has adopted her unconditionally.[7]

"Would you feel comfortable being close to Him, even being held by Him?"

"No—I don't think so. It just seems like that is too informal, you know?"

"You're doing great. Do you still sense Jesus' presence with you?"

[Nods.]

"Great. Would you like to ask Jesus if He would take you to the Father? That's part of the reason He came to earth in the first place."

"Okay . . . Jesus, will You show me Father? Oh, I'm seeing a garden and Jesus and I are walking. It feels cool out."

"Do you see Father God?"

"Yes, He's over there."

She points like we can see, too. She is *very* visual, and Jesus is meeting her now. It feels foolish, but here we go. I'm nervous, but who cares?

"Would you like to ask Jesus a question?"

"Okay."

"Ask: 'Jesus, can I go see Papa God?' [Pause.] What's happening? What are you seeing, sensing or feeling right now?"

"I am in His lap. Oh, He has such clear twinkling eyes."

Long pause. Some giggles. I can't wait to hear what's happening.

My wife smiles.

I tear up.

"Want to ask Him a brave question?"

"Sure, I like Him."

"Ask this then: 'Papa God, what do You think of me?'"

[Pause.]

"He says I'm cool and He likes hanging with me because I'm fun, too—like Him. That's strange, I never thought about God actually liking me, or being fun-loving like me, too!"

"How does that sound to you?"

"Well, I'm not bragging or anything, but He is God so it must be true, you know? Is that okay to think that?"

"How does it feel to you right now?"

"I would never make that stuff up. It is not at all what I thought just a minute ago."

We sit and savor for a few minutes. She opens her eyes and says she wants to share a couple more things before she leaves. It's clear to us that her time in Papa's lap opened the door to get really clean.

Click.

We do a little spring cleaning using the "Four Doors" tool, probing four key areas of her life and "Doing Kingdom Business": fear, hatred and unforgiveness, sexual sin and soul ties, and occult and false religion. Just cleaning up some debris. It felt good to her to get stuff out of all the corners.

"One thing that I want to share is that my boyfriend and I have been . . . well . . . you know. It's sort of embarrassing."

"Would you like only my wife to be with you right now? That's fine with me."

"No. It's okay. It's not like you don't know or anything."

She shares just enough so we know; no more details are necessary. We lead her in confession of that relationship. She suddenly sees that she was using him for security. She repents of that and proclaims,

"I give back to Jimmy the part of his heart that he gave to me when we had sex. And I take back from him now the part of my heart I gave to him before the right time. I break now that soul tie that is not from God. I'm sorry, Papa God, for taking the place of a wife with Your son Jimmy—I hurt him and Your heart. Jesus, please teach me how to really love. It will be hard, I may mess up, but tonight I choose to do it right."

It feels good to be able to say, like Jesus, "He has nothing in Me."[8]

We blessed her long and good. We spoke about her destiny as being a great and cool friend and so capable—we had seen that in her for weeks. She swelled with inner pride—the good kind.

We reminded her of the things that had happened that night—of the new relationships, of the lies and liars sent packing, of her pictures of Papa that were a gift to her, of the fact that when she confessed, Jesus took it all.

We spoke briefly about talking to her boyfriend about what happened at the right time and about setting appropriate boundaries. She had an older friend who would help them, she said.

We sensed things for that day were complete. My wife and I unsnapped the tool belt, hung it on the hook next to our bed and laid down. Lying there, I wept for joy at the goodness of God.

What a cool hobby I have, restoring lives. Thank You, Papa. When I feel You put Your hands on mine, it is wonderful.

Two weeks later as I sat in the living room, Betsy bounded up the porch steps all bubbly and smiling.

"Guess what?"

"What?"

"I am sooo happy!"

"You are!"

"And know what else?"

"What?"

"I have girlfriends. And they think I'm cool. We're going bowling together. What a hoot."

I smile.

"Know what else, Mr. Reese? I *am* cool!"

A hug and a kiss and out the door.

What could possibly be more fun?

Is everything in her young life perfectly straight? No, not till she is in heaven. Just like you and me. But many things have changed for her. We check in from time to time, and she has friends who know how to help her walk out her freedom. She is no longer prisoner to the lie that had bound her boundless energy and joy, and she no longer is afraid of Papa God. She no longer has the *obligation* to feel miserable, though still the *opportunity*. But now she has a choice.

It has been two years now. She is married to Jimmy and has a child. She is at peace with her family and especially intimate with God. She is helping a couple of single moms find the intimacy they lacked growing up—with her favorite Papa.

Your Turn

> Seeing the people, He felt compassion for them, because they were distressed and dispirited like sheep without a shepherd. Then He said to His disciples, "The harvest is plentiful, but the workers are few. Therefore beseech the Lord of the harvest to send out workers into His harvest."
>
> Matthew 9:36–38

This Scripture is often used for evangelism. But there is a more specific application illustrated here. The wording is very graphic. It literally says the people were "fleeced, mangled and cast to the ground in abject depression and despair." It sounds for all the world like coming on the aftermath of a wolf attack. And, it says, Jesus was moved deeply within Himself with compassion—His "bowels" ached. And His response is to tell His disciples to cry out to the Lord for people to be moved with compassion, equipped and willing to minister to that condition.

That is us.

In our world today some things are not that great. In U.S. society, one of the richest places on earth, a record 37 percent of all babies are born out of wedlock, and among women ages 20 to 24, the statistic is approaching half. Half of all babies without nuclear families. Only one-third of all marriages will reach their 25th anniversary—and the percentage of married people is at an all-time low: 59 percent. Almost 11 percent of all students will drop out of high school in any one year. Recreational marijuana and habitual drug use of deadly methamphetamine and Ecstasy are at epidemic levels. Downcast, dispirited, mangled, depressed, alone and abandoned.

That is us, too.

Perhaps this is why God says, in the last verse of the Old Testament, that one sign of the end times, one thing that will be desperately needed is turning the hearts of the fathers to the children and the hearts of the children to the fathers.[9]

It is your turn now, you know. You know too much to turn back now. It is your turn to be healed and freed; your turn to heal and free others; your turn to play with Papa God and His amazing Son; and your turn to be humble and brave and to walk with the Holy Spirit.

Jesus is still watching over His sheep and seeing their sorry condition, and He is still asking Papa for harvester-shepherds who are willing to risk it with Him. He is asking for you—but you know that or you would not have read this book to the end.

I beseech You, Lord, to look on this one who is reading this. I ask You to encourage them that they will smile the smile of young King David who ran to the giant, confident in the victory, angry that someone could so frighten and dismay God's people. I ask You to give them comrades and teammates. Most of all, I ask You to let them play with You, to be in Your yoke with You and to be more and more in love with You, in awe of You, that You would choose to use such as them.

Amen, and thank You, Papa.

Notes

Chapter 1 Polite Society

1. Proverbs 4:18; Isaiah 61:1; 2 Corinthians 3:18; Galatians 6:1; James 5:16; 1 John 1:7.

2. Interestingly, in the same way, but on the negative side, Scripture uses a single Greek word (*peirasmos*) to describe both demonic temptations and demonic tests. Temptation is designed to *lure* us to destruction through bad choices and make us prisoners; demonic trials are designed to *push* us to destruction. It is all from one source, with one deadly aim.

3. 1 Thessalonians 5:23.

4. Proverbs 4:23.

5. John 8:32.

6. Check out our website (thefreedomresource.org) and its links.

Chapter 2 Two Foundations about God

1. Gregory Boyd, *God at War* (Downers Grove, Ill.: InterVarsity Press, 1997), 32.

2. Acts 17:6.

3. William Coffin, interviewed by Terry Gross, *Fresh Air*, WHYY Radio, April 14, 2006.

4. John 16:33, NKJV.

5. John 15:19; Galatians 1:4; 1 John 4:4; 5:19.

6. Luke 15.

7. John 8:34–36.

8. Isaiah 53:4; Luke 4:18.

9. Romans 8:29; 2 Timothy 1:9; 1 Peter 1:3–5.

10. Philippians 1:6; 2 Timothy 1:12.

11. Hebrews 12:2.

12. Philippians 2:12–13.

13. Judges 6:1.

14. Acts 9:1.

15. Matthew 10:30.

16. Psalm 139:16.

17. Psalm 139:17–18.

18. "Father's Love Letter," *Father Heart Communications*, copyright 1999–2006, www.FathersLoveLetter.com, used by permission.

Chapter 3 Two Foundations about Our Enemy

1. Tertullian, *The Apology*, trans. S. Thelwall (Whitefish, Mont.: Kessinger Publishing), chap. 23.

2. Mark 5:9; Matthew 17:18; Acts 16:18.

3. Matthew 16:23, kjv.

4. Some more examples include: Psalm 101:3; Luke 9:54; 22:31; John 8:43; 13:2; Acts 5:3; 1 Corinthians 10:20; 2 Corinthians 4:3; 11:3, 13; Ephesians 2:1; 1 Timothy 3:6; 5:14; Hebrews 2:14; James 3:14; 1 John 5:19.

5. John 16:33, nkjv.

6. God the Father works through Jesus by the Holy Spirit. All are shown in Scripture to be mutually involved, concerned and active. They are one. We can address any of the Trinity in a ministry time. Many find it easiest to speak to Jesus, as they can picture and relate most easily to Him.

7. 1 Corinthians 1:25.

8. Psalm 139:16; John 5:19; Romans 12:3; Ephesians 2:10; Hebrews 2:24.

9. 2 Corinthians 3:18.

10. Ephesians 4:7, 11–12, 15–16.

11. Ezekiel 28:11–19.

Chapter 4 Two Foundations about Us

1. 2 Samuel 21:1; Joshua 9.

2. Matthew 22:31.

3. Matthew 22:24; 26:33.

4. Matthew 7:1–2.

5. Matthew 27:3–6; John 12:6.

6. John 5:14.

7. Colossians 3:25.

8. Mark 10:30; Colossians 3:23–25; 1 Timothy 5:24.

9. 1 Corinthians 3:13–15.

10. Luke 4:18.

11. Matthew 18:34–35.

12. John 14:23.

13. Proverbs 4:23.

14. Based on the insights of Dr. Ed Smith and Doris and Peter Wagner.

15. That is why, in dealing with younger children, the two most common forms of "Doing Kingdom Business" are helping children learn how to combat fear and how to walk in forgiveness.

Chapter 5 Two Foundations about Being a First Responder

1. Exodus 3.

2. 1 Corinthians 3:9.

3. Idea courtesy of Bob Mumford.

4. Isaiah 55:8–9; 1 Corinthians 1:20–25.

5. John 5:19, among others.

6. John 10:1–5.

7. John 7:37.

8. Thanks to Mark Virkler and Communion with God Ministries at http://www.cwgministries.org.

9. Thanks to Diane Hawkins for the basis of this analogy.

10. Luke 18:18–27.

11. John 4:19–24.

12. 2 Corinthians 10:1; Galatians 6:1; Philippians 2:1–2; Colossians 3:12; 2 Timothy 2:25; 1 Peter 3:15; James 3:13.

13. 1 Corinthians 14:3.

Chapter 6 Two Foundations about Tools and Process

1. See also Deuteronomy 23:21–23 and Matthew 12:33–37 for more on "mere words."

2. Gail Saltz, *Becoming Real* (New York: Riverhead, 2004), 5.

3. 2 Corinthians 3:18.

Chapter 7 Key Elements

1. Hebrews 11:6; James 1:6–7.

2. Proverbs 25:11–12; Matthew 18:15; Galatians 6:1–2.

3. 2 Corinthians 5:17; Romans 6:1–6.

4. Matthew 5:23–24; 7:1–2; Luke 17:3–4; 1 Corinthians 4:5.

5. Deuteronomy 21:21–23; Proverbs 18:7; Matthew 5:35–37; 12:36–37.

6. There is much more to say about generational curses and structures of iniquity and about prenatal issues. Please refer to www.thefreedomresource.org for more information and links.

7. Romans 5–8.

8. Psalm 32:1–6; 13:21; James 5:19–20; 1 John 1:8–9; 2:1.

9. Biblical restitution is restoring what they have taken and then some in order to allow the other person to trust us again and to help restore normal relationship. See Exodus 22 for more on this.

10. 2 Corinthians 5:18–19.

11. http://www.healinghouse.org/index.html.

12. For example, Romans 1:18–2:11; 2 Corinthians 4:3–4; 1 Timothy 4:1–3; Hebrews 3:12–4:9.

Chapter 8 Putting It Together

1. God the Father works through Jesus by the Holy Spirit. We can address any of the Trinity in a session. Many find it easiest to speak to Jesus, as they can picture and relate most easily to Him. We will use the term "Jesus" throughout, though Papa God and the Holy Spirit are equally loving, concerned and involved.

2. Psalms 22:10; 58:3; Proverb 18:14; Luke 1:44.

3. 2 Corinthians 1:3–5; 1 Peter 5:6–7.

4. Matthew 7:1–5; Colossians 3:12–13.

5. Proverbs 18:21; Matthew 12:33–37.

6. Psalm 109:28; Luke 6:28.

7. Proverbs 26:2.

8. Leviticus 26:40–42; Matthew 23:34–36; Romans 5:12–21; Galatians 3:13–14.

9. Psalm 32:1–6; Matthew 5:23–24; 1 John 1:8–9.

10. A great source of condensed truth can be found in Neil Anderson's books.

11. John 8:32.

12. Matthew 12:43–45.

13. 1 Corinthians 15:33.

14. 2 Timothy 2:22.

15. Philippians 2:12–13.

16. Matthew 18:10.

17. Stephen Arterburn and Fred Stoeker, *Every Young Man's Battle: Strategies for Victory in the Real World of Sexual Temptation* (Colorado Springs: Water-Brook, 2002).

18. 1 Corinthians 6:18; 2 Timothy 2:22.

19. My friend tells this story on his wife—and it is way funnier when he tells it.

20. 2 Timothy 1:7.

Chapter 9 Dealing with Demons

1. See, for example, the books and other materials of Peter Horrobin, Don Basham, Neil Anderson, Bob Larson, Derek Prince, Jessie Penn Lewis, Charles Kraft and Ed Smith. We in Sozo ministry owe these men and women a debt of gratitude for their enlightened examples and clear writings, and I want to acknowledge them here.

2. Luke 4:13.

3. The term "spiritual warfare" is a bit of a misnomer since Jesus has won the war. But Paul does talk about struggle and that is the term we will use.

4. Revelation 12:9–10.

5. 1 Timothy 4:1.

6. John 10:10.

7. John 8:44.

8. Mark 5:9.

9. Acts 16:16–17.

10. For example, there is a theory called the "gap theory" that demons are disembodied spirits of a pre-Adamic race.

11. Deuteronomy 32:16; Psalm 106:37; 1 Corinthians 10:20.

12. Mark 5:12.

13. Mark 5:1–13.

14. It is interesting that the final result of that manifestation of the demons was that hundreds of scared people repented of their evil practices and burned their magic books. God is a better chess player than Satan!

15. Analogy thanks to Kris Valatton, Bethel Church, Redding, California.

16. Stalling or avoiding is a demonic tactic. "If you refuse . . . " is used throughout this tool in making the demons come to a decision point where they clearly obey or know they are in opposition to the direct authority of Jesus and will have to deal with Him and/or His angels. It is an idea we learned from Dr. Ed Smith that we have often found effective.

17. Mark 9:15–29.

18. See, for example, Jude 1:8–9 for the *wrong* attitude.

19. Hebrews 4:15.

20. We will use our buddy Bob throughout the chapter but will only hit the key phrases or conclusions of the ministry conversation.

21. Ephesians 4:27.

22. For example, "You spirit that took advantage of John's jealousy . . ."

23. Isaiah 14:12–17; Ezekiel 28:17–19; Mark 16:17; Luke 10:18–19; 11:20; Acts 10:38; Colossians 2:15; Hebrews 2:14–15; Revelation 12:11; 20:10.

24. Mark 9:25.

25. A follow-up audio called *Winning the Daily Battle* is available from http://www.thefreedomresource.org.

Chapter 10 The Four Doors

1. See Carlos Annacondia and Gisela Sawin, *Listen to Me, Satan! Exercising Authority over the Devil in Jesus' Name*, ed. Caribe and Betania (Lake Mary, Fla.: Charisma House, 1997). Another great approach that checks open doors is that of Neil Anderson. For more information, see http://www.ficm.org.

2. See, for example, 2 Corinthians 11:19–20 and Galatians 2:4–5 for church-based soul ties.

3. 1 Thessalonians 4:16.

4. 1 Corinthians 6:16.

5. See, for example, Ted Roberts, *Pure Desire* (Regal); Patrick Carnes, *Out of the Shadows* (Hazeldon); Harry W. Schaumburg, *False Intimacy* (NavPress); Stephen Arterburn, et al., *Every Man's Battle* (WaterBrook); David Cross, *Soul Ties* (Sovereign World); Jill Southern, *Sex* (Sovereign World). See also resources on my friend David Kyle Foster's website: http://masteringlife.gospelcom.net, especially for homosexual issues.

6. 2 Timothy 2:22.

7. 1 Corinthians 9:27.

8. 1 Thessalonians 4:4.

9. Ephesians 6:1–3.

10. 2 Corinthians 11:2–3.

11. 2 Corinthians 11:13, 20.

12. Interestingly, recent brain scan studies on newer, more potent forms of marijuana show that the active ingredient THC shuts down the part of the brain that protects or modulates irrational and hallucinatory thoughts.

Chapter 11 The Father Ladder

1. Luke 15. The prodigal, the older brother, the lost sheep and the lost coin all ended in undeserved parties!

2. Romans 8:15; Galatians 4:6. A Hebrew childlike term of endearment equivalent to Daddy, Papa or even Pops in English.

3. The "Father Ladder" was conceived in its present form by Alan Ray, late of Bethel Church in Redding, California. It has been significantly modified by Dawna DeSilva, also from Bethel.

4. This is a condensed fictitious account showing the key points in a typical session. In reality there may be many more questions and exchanges to get to the closing point. Any similarity between this example and any specific real-life Sozo session is coincidental. Another tool may be appropriate as well, but we will limit ourselves to this tool and "Doing Kingdom Business."

Chapter 12 Presenting Jesus

1. See, for example, http://www.listeningprayer.ca.

2. Interestingly, a couple of my counseling friends pointed out that some of the basic understanding comes from, or is shared with, the cognitive therapy approaches—with the twist that God Himself, not a counselor or the counselee, brings truth.

3. For more information, see the Theophostic Prayer Ministry website at http://www.theophostic.com.

4. We are indebted to the ideas, insights and approaches found in a number of Christian and even other sources. It must be stated that this tool, while containing elements from many sources, is not from or created by these ministries.

5. For a very interesting discussion of brains and memory, see Daniel Gilbert, *Stumbling on Happiness* (Random House, 2005).

6. See http://www.amethysthealingconcepts.com for more information on this subject.

7. This is a condensed fictitious account showing the key points in a typical session. In reality there may be many more questions and exchanges to get to the closing point. Observe the flow of the Fruit Loop. Any similarity between this example and any specific real-life Sozo session is coincidental. Another tool may be appropriate as well, but we will limit ourselves to this tool and "Doing Kingdom Business" and "Dealing with Demons."

Epilogue

1. John 8:44.
2. Mark 11:25.
3. James 4:7–8.
4. Matthew 11:28–30.
5. John 17:11–19; 1 Corinthians 10:13.
6. Psalm 139:17–18; Matthew 10:30.
7. John 14:2–5; Romans 8:15.
8. John 14:30.
9. Malachi 4:6.

Index

abandonment, 75
abuse, 39, 162
addiction, 75, 76
adversity, 22
Alcoholics Anonymous, 25
alternative medicines, 191
Anderson, Neil, 244n1
angels, 157
anger, 178, 183–86
anorexia, 76
authority, 61, 156, 157–59, 163, 171–72,
   173
avoiding, 245n16

barriers, 137
Basham, Don, 244n1
behavior, 27
beliefs, 26–27, 85
binding and releasing, 173
blessing, 143, 224
bondage, 71, 75, 180–81
bonding, 181
boot step, 113, 133, 137–41, 146–50
   and demons, 170–74
   and fear and control, 188
   and occult, 191–92
   and soul ties, 182–83
   and unforgiveness, 186

brains, 27
brokenness, 27

captives, 71, 72–78
casting out demons, 170–74
cause and effect, 66–69
celebration, 111
child abuse, 29
children, dealing with, 242n15
cleansing, 124
Coffin, William Sloan, 37–38
cognitive therapy approaches, 246n2
   (chap. 12)
compassion, 41, 238
confession of sin, 21, 54, 62, 124
confusion, 75
consequences, of sin, 68
control, 178, 186–88
coping mechanisms, 76
core lies, 74, 126
counseling, 25, 87
covenant, 66
co-workers with God, 80
culture of honor, 89–93

darkness, 138–39
David, 66

247

"Dealing with Demons" tool, 101, 153–75, 186, 188, 191, 232–33
death, 97
deception, 56
declaring and choosing, 173
defense mechanisms, 76, 117
deliverance, 122, 124, 125, 169
demonic influence, 29, 83, 133, 241n2 (chap. 1)
demonology, 153
demons, 48–52, 74, 76–77, 100, 111, 133, 140–41, 241n2 (chap. 1). See also "Dealing with Demons" tool
denominationalism, 191
dependence, on God, 25
dependency relationships, 180, 182
destiny, 42, 56–57, 58, 85, 103
devil, 59, 140–41
Diagnostic and Statistical Manual of Mental Disorders IV, 23
disaffirmation, 75
dissociation, 29, 162
divination, 191
"Doing Kingdom Business" (DKB), 100, 113–15, 182, 186, 188, 191, 192, 232
domestic violence, 29
DWD. See "Dealing with Demons" tool

emotions, 15, 23, 115–16, 219–20
entanglements, 100, 109–10, 114, 122–23, 132, 133, 138–39
environment, 145
evil, 36, 157
evil spirits, 157. See also demons

faith, 85, 143
false religion, 178, 189–92
fate, 19–20, 58
"Father Ladder" tool, 101, 140, 201–14, 234–36
fear, 55–56, 74, 162, 178, 186–88, 242n15
first aid for the soul, 24, 28
flow of God, 217
forgiveness, 54, 57, 116, 117–22, 141–42, 232, 242n15
foundations, 28–29

"Four Doors" tool, 101, 177–200, 236
framing the truth, 127
freedom, 16, 17, 25, 71, 78, 85, 238
    and demons, 154
    and forgiveness, 117, 120
    and will of God, 41–46
free will, 38–39
friendships, 17
Fruit Loop, 29, 100, 112–13, 115, 132, 145–50, 164, 178
fruit step, 113, 127, 133, 134–35, 145–50
    and demons, 164–66
    and fear and control, 188
    and occult, 191
    and soul ties, 182
    and unforgiveness, 185

gap theory, 244n10 (chap. 9)
God. See also Papa God
    compassion of, 41
    as Father, 202–3
    gentle humor of, 85
    goodness of, 36–41
    love of, 43–46, 72
    as mysterious and capricious, 35
    presence of, 72
    sovereignty of, 40
    voice of, 82–86
grieving the Spirit, 91

habitual sin, 124
healing, 17
heart, 85
hidden enemies, 53–58
Holy Spirit, 243n1 (chap. 8)
    and demonic manifestations, 161
    quenching and grieving of, 90–91
    refilling of, 174
    on sonship, 202
homosexuality, 76
honor, 89–93, 185
hope, 57, 143
hopelessness, 75
Horrobin, Peter, 244n1
humans, complexity of, 29

identity, 75, 85
idolatry, 192
imagination and impression, 84–85, 87–88
infilling from God, 141–42
information, 61
inner healing, 22, 25, 126, 169, 217
insight, 83
inspiration, 83
intention, 61, 63
invasion, of sin, 73
issues, not random, 59–63

Jesus
  compassion of, 238
  death and resurrection of, 158–59
  and the Father, 81–82
  as picture of God, 39–41
  spoke to and listened to demons, 169
Johnson, Bill, 36
Joshua, 66
joy, 143
judgment, 118–19
justice, 174

kingdom. *See* "Doing Kingdom Business"
Kraft, Charles, 244n1
Kylstra, Chester and Betsy, 126

Larson, Bob, 244n1
"lay" approach, 25
leadership, 60
legitimacy, of relationships, 181
Lewis, Jesse Penn, 244n1
lies, 74, 137, 142–43, 156
life, 97
lifestyle, sinful, 164
Lion King, The (film), 79–80
listening, 134
listening prayer, 217
loot step, 113, 133, 141–44, 146–50
  and demons, 174–75
  and fear and control, 188
  and occult, 192
  and soul ties, 183
  and unforgiveness, 186

lost coin parable, 109, 119, 133
lost sheep parable, 109–10, 132, 133

manifestations, of demonic, 160–61
Matrix, The (film), 216
measure of God, 58
meekness, 62
memory, 84–85, 87–88, 221–24
mental health professionals, 23
mental illness, 29
metron, 58–59
Moses, 80

New Age, 191
Newton, Isaac, 65–66

occult, 178, 189–92
older brother story, 110–11, 133
origin, and outcome, 39

pain, 34–36, 219–21
Papa God, 16–17, 25, 127–28, 203, 205–7, 234–36, 239, 243n1 (chap. 8)
partners with God, 78, 80–88
personal tainting, 75
polite society, 20–21
prayer, 115–16
predestination, 42
"Presenting Jesus" tool, 101, 137, 140, 215–28, 230–31
Prince, Derek, 244n1
prisoners, 71, 72–78
process, 96, 101–3
prodigal son parable, 110, 132, 133
prophecy, 91, 222–23
providence, 57

quenching the Spirit, 90–91

rebellion, 139–40
rebuking the devil and demons, 140–41
reclaiming lost ground, 174
reconciliation, 125
referral, 162–63
rejection, 75
rejoicing, 112
relationships, 24, 61, 85, 181

renouncing, 138–39
repeat-after-me prayers, 115–16, 233
repentance, 110, 120–21, 124, 139–40
retribution, 119
revelation, 61
ritualized actions, 76
root step, 113, 127, 133, 135–36,
    145–50
    and demons, 166–70
    and fear and control, 188
    and occult, 191
    and soul ties, 182
    and unforgiveness, 185–86

Saltz, Gail, 98–99
Satan, 39, 52, 59, 66–67, 155
Saul, 66
scoot step, 113, 128, 133, 144–45,
    146–50, 224
    and demons, 175
    and fear and control, 188
    and occult, 192
    and soul ties, 183
    and unforgiveness, 186
self-control, 165
senses and drives, 84–85
sexual sin, 178, 179–83
shame, 75
Simon Peter, 66
sin, 68, 73, 75, 100, 110, 139–40, 182
sin issues, 123–26, 132, 133
Smith, Ed, 217, 244n1
sorcery, 191
soul ties, 178, 179–83, 236
sowing and reaping, 67
Sozo, 16, 24–26
spiritual struggle, 155

spiritual warfare, 244n3 (chap. 9)
stalling, 245n16
stories, 99
stress, 22, 53
strongholds, 74, 76, 112, 155, 168,
    217–18
suicide, 29, 55

temptation, 72, 155, 241n2 (chap. 1)
Tertullian, 49
tools, 95–101
traumatic incident, 168
tribulation, 53
Trinity, 243n1 (chap. 8)
truth, 127–28, 140, 142–43

unbelief system, 171
unconscious, 98–99
unforgiveness, 178, 183–86
ungodly beliefs, 100, 110–11, 126–28,
    133, 140

van Gogh, Vincent, 54–57
vengeance, 119
victimization, 74–75
violence, 162
visualization, 87–88
voice of God, 82–86

WESUD, 29, 100, 102, 108–12, 132,
    135, 178
wholeness, 20
WIGO, 134
will of God, 37–38, 41–46
witchcraft, 190
words, power of, 97
wounding, 76, 100, 109, 133, 156

Andrew (Andy) J. Reese has served as an active minister and church leader for many years with a focus on the areas of inner healing and deliverance. He is the president of The Freedom Resource (www.thefreedomresource.org), a ministry dedicated to providing training, networking and information using the Sozo ministry model. He has led and participated on teams that have taught this method in various settings both nationally and internationally. He is a noted speaker, writer and leader with many years of experience in church leadership and Christian inner healing, counseling and deliverance. He also pursues a successful career in engineering and management consulting.

For more information about Andy Reese and Sozo, visit the Freedom Resource website.